Decently
and in
Good Order

Decently and in Good Order

THE CHURCH ORDER OF THE CANADIAN AND AMERICAN REFORMED CHURCHES

as revised by the General Synods

Cloverdale 1983

and

Burlington-West 1986

commented on by

G. VAN RONGEN

and

K. DEDDENS

PREMIER PUBLISHING — WINNIPEG

Van Rongen, G., 1918-
  Decently and in good order

  ISBN 0-88756-034-2
1. Reformed Church — Canada — Government.
2. Church orders, Reformed. I. Deddens, K. II. Title.
BX9598.Z5V25 1987   285.7'71   C87-098016-5

Acknowledgment:
                  The Standing Committee for the Publication of the
                  Book of Praise of the Canadian Reformed Churches
                  kindly granted us permission to include the text of
                  the Church Order.

Cover illustration: A. Schiebaan, Kelmscott, Western Australia

PREMIER PUBLISHING
1249 PLESSIS ROAD, WINNIPEG, MANITOBA, CANADA R2C 3L9

Preface

Several churches of Reformed origin have in the course of times adopted "the Church Order of Dordrecht" and amended it according to the circumstances under which they were living. One of the latest revisions is that which in recent years was undertaken by the Canadian Reformed Churches.

This important event created a good opportunity to write and publish a brief commentary.

Herein the example set within the Free Reformed Churches of Australia is followed.

A brief commentary on the Church Order of these churches was introduced as a "textbook" at the Theological College at Hamilton.

However, while the Church Order of the sister churches in Australia and that of the churches in Canada and the United States of America are fundamentally identical, there are a number of variations. This led to the idea to re-write the Australian edition for the Canadian/American situation, and make this edition available to the members of the Canadian Reformed Churches.

This may explain the fact that this present publication carries the names of two authors.

The name of the second one may be accepted as natural: he has been charged with the commission to lecture on Church Polity at the Theological College.

The bearer of the first name is the author of the "Australian" commentary. With some boldness he agrees with the use of the phrase "our Church Order" since he had the privilege of spending a number of years in the midst of the Canadian Reformed Churches as a minister of the American Reformed Church at Grand Rapids, Michigan.

Our commentary is a brief one only. This leaves room for the publication of a broader work.

The latest alterations made by the General Synod Burlington-West 1986 have been included.

We hope our work may serve the edification of the Churches.

Kelmscott, Western Australia
Hamilton, Ontario   *October, 1986.*

Contents

IV. Worship, Sacraments, and Ceremonies

V. Christian Discipline

Preliminary Remarks

1. "All things should be done decently and in order."
More than once this apostolic command, given in I Corinthians 14:40, was included in the early Church Orders of the churches of the Reformation.

Our present Order refers to it also. The words "good order" in Articles 1, 16, and 45 are obviously an abbreviation of the phrase "decently and in good order" in Article 22.

These references prove that adopting a Church Order is a serious business, while at the same time it expresses the intention and desire to be a true apostolic church.

2. What actually is a Church Order?
In the year 1561 such a document was published for the Reformed church at Geneva, its title being *Ordonnances Ecclésiastiques* — ecclesiastical ordinances.

The introduction considers it to be essential that

> the doctrine of the holy Gospel of our Lord shall be preserved in its purity, and that the Christian church be maintained by a sound government and police, and that also the youth be well and faithfully instructed in the things which have to be done . . . and which cannot be done without a certain fixed rule and manner, from which everyone can learn the duty of his particular office.
>
> Therefore it seemed to be useful that the spiritual government which our Lord has shown us and has instituted by His Word, would be moulded in a good form, so that it would have a place among us and be observed by us.

This is fundamentally the same as what Marnix of St. Aldegonde wrote when the very first synod of the churches in the Netherlands had been convened at Emden in the year 1571. He said that it would be useful

> to establish some fixed and unchangeable agreements with each other, not only in the chapters of the pure doctrine but also in the manners, ceremonies, and government of the churches; also to have communion and good understanding with each other, so that the churches may be able to diligently hear about each other's condition and situation and assist each other in all the current affairs.

3. "Emden" did indeed compile a Church Order.
It was based upon the Order the Reformed churches in France had adopted in the year 1559.

We mention the latter because it informs us about another aspect of the nature of a Church Order:

This French Church Order was the sequel to the Confession of Faith the Reformed churches in that country had adopted earlier in the same year.

Immediately after the last article of the Confession the title of the Church Order was printed. It read:

> Concerning Church discipline, here is a first outline of its essentials as they are contained in the apostolic writings.

A good Reformed Church Order claims to show how the Lord Jesus rules His church and how He desires it to be governed. It summarizes what the apostles have spoken and written regarding church discipline and good order, and applies it to the present circumstances. In this respect it is an elaboration on certain articles of the Confession of Faith.

K. Schilder once wrote (*Tolle Lege* I, 1952, p.98):

> The Church Order develops certain principles; even Church politics are a matter of doctrine.

And also this (*Tolle Lege* II, 1954, p.19):

> The church does not start from principles, but from the revelation of these principles.

A good Church Order is based on God's Word.

4. We would like to illustrate the confessional nature of a Scriptural Church Order by quoting a few lines from *The Form of Presbyterial Church Government* as it was drafted at Westminster in the year 1645 and afterwards was adopted by the church of Scotland.

It is true, our own Church Order and the Presbyterian Form are different. Yet, the following words, which have been taken from "The Preface," may be helpful to give us a good insight into the character of a good Church Order. Here they are:

> Jesus Christ, upon whose shoulders the government is, whose name is called Wonderful, Counsellor, the mighty God, the everlasting Father, the Prince of Peace (1), of the increase of whose government and peace there should be no end; who sits upon the throne of David, and upon his kingdom, to order it, and to establish it with judgement and justice, from henceforth, ever for ever; having all power given unto him in heaven and in earth by the Father, who raised him from the dead, and set him at his own right hand, far above all principalities and power, and might, and dominion, and every name that is named, not only in this world, but also in that which is to come, and put all things under his feet, and gave him to be head over all things to the church, which is his body, the fullness of him that filleth all in all: he being ascended up far above all heavens, that he might

fill all things, received gifts for his church, and gave officers, necessary for the edification of his church, and perfecting of his saints (2).

1 — Isa.IX.6,7.
2 — Matt.XXVIII.18,19.20. Eph.I.20,21,22,23. Cf.Eph. IV.8,11, and Ps.LXVIII.18.

Here it is clearly stated: the Lord Jesus Christ rules and governs His church from heaven, using the service of men, who were given to Him by the Father as spoils of war, according to Ephesians 4:11.

5. This chapter, Ephesians 4, starts by referring to the unity of the Christian church (verses 4 - 6):

> There is one body and one Spirit, just as you were called to the one hope that belongs to your call, one Lord, one faith, one baptism, one God and Father of us all, who is above all and through all and in all.

This unity, then, has to be maintained and shown (verses 1 and 3):

> I therefore, a prisoner for the Lord, beg you to lead a life worthy of the calling to which you have been called . . . eager to maintain the unity of the Spirit in the bond of peace.

This duty, which was so clearly explained to the congregations at Ephesus and its surroundings, is still the same in our days. As local congregations we shall show and maintain our "unity in the Spirit."

This, then, has been acknowledged by our Reformed churches. In Article 32 of the Belgic Confession of Faith they state:

> It is useful and good for those who govern the Church to establish a certain order to maintain the body of the Church.

Our Church Order is, indeed, a set of ordinances for maintaining the body of the church, in the unity of true faith. It has been anchored in Holy Scripture and in the Confession.

A good Church Order is essential for the bond of churches, created by the Lord Jesus: In His royal messages in the initial chapters of the Book of Revelation He uses the plural:

> He, who has an ear, let him hear what the Spirit says to the churches.

6. In the "good old days" the contents of Article 74 — which can today be found near the end of the Church Order — appeared as Article 1, besides which it was also slightly longer. It now reads:

> No Church shall in any way lord it over other Churches, no office-bearer over other office-bearers.

In the sixteenth century, however, it was thus formulated (in our translation):

No church shall in any way lord it over another church, no minister of the Word, no elder, no deacon shall lord it over another one, but everyone shall be on his guard against any suspicion and temptation to lord it over others.

It may be clear that here again the confessional character of the Reformed Church Order is expressed. It says as it were: We are no Roman Catholics, but have been granted the grace of returning to the Scriptural government of the church, to the one and only universal Bishop and the only Head of the church, our Lord and Saviour Jesus Christ. Therefore no congregation is more important, and no office bearer is a higher authority than any other.

Even apart from this, the strong emphasis put on this particular article proves that right from the beginning the great "Reformed principle" was formulated: the federation of churches is a matter of a voluntary act of free churches in accordance with what Holy Scripture states concerning the unity of the Spirit to be maintained. They have agreed to do certain things in the same way; to support each other in several respects; to have mutual supervision over each other in order that they may continue to be true and faithful churches of the Lord Jesus Christ; to create a certain form of jurisdiction in their midst; and to undertake a number of common activities, e.g. regarding the training for the Ministry of the Word.

Summarizing all this we can say: Our Reformed Church Orde is of an anti-hierarchical character — no pope, no synodocracy —, it is at the same time anti-dependentism.

7. Christ Jesus, Whom we confess as the only universal Bishop and the only Head of the church (Article 31, Belgic Confession of Faith) gathers, defends, and preserves her by His Spirit and Word (Lord's Day 21, Heidelberg Catechism).

We further believe that His church "must be governed to the Spiritual order which our Lord has taught in His Word" (Article 30 Belgic Confession of Faith).

A brief exposition of this order is given in Articles 30-31 of that Confession.

Comparing the main contents of our Church Order — as e.g. indicated in Article 1 — with Articles 30-32 of the Belgic Confession, we come to the conclusion that this document is a further exposition of what our churches confess on the ground of God's Word.

It is true, a number of clauses included in the Church Order are nothing more than agreements between the churches to handle certain matters in an identical fashion, where in fact different paths could be chosen. Also contained in our Church Order are several stipulations which cannot be traced back to any commandment of Christ or His apostles, yet they were laid down as being beneficial to the churches in showing unity and presenting a common front. We may refer here e.g. to Articles 32, 43, and 44c. Apart from that, it is not a kind of code, containing all kinds of detailed rules and regulations.

However, generally speaking our Church Order is based on the "Spiritual order" which we are taught in the Scriptures.

It is therefore an important element in maintaining the unity of faith among the churches and in each local congregation.

This does not mean that our Church Order is a perfect document. It goes without saying that neither creeds, confessions, nor church orders ever attain equal level with Holy Scripture; if ever anything in them is recognized as being incorrect or wrong, they must be amended. The late Professor P. Deddens of the Kampen Theological Seminary used to say: "To have a Church Order is a good thing, but only together with an open Bible!"

However, it is incorrect and very demeaning to hold to the belief that the Church Order, having been compiled by men, need not to be taken too seriously.

8. The Church Order of Dordrecht — we owe it to the well-known (inter)national Synod of Dordrecht, 1618/19 — did not just fall from the air.

We have already made mention of the Church Order of Emden, 1571.

However, the very first preparations were made at the Convention of Wesel, 1568. They resulted in the publication of the so-called "Articles of Wesel."

After "Emdem," other synods also had to deal with the Church Order, and on some of those occasions it was revised and/or extended. The Dutch churches had to learn by experience!

We mention here the names of the Provincial Synod of Dordrecht, 1574; of the National Synod of Dordrecht, 1578; of the National Synod of Middelburg, 1581; and that of The Hague, 1586.

The Synod of Dordrecht, 1618/19, did not only produce the Canons of Dort, but also thoroughly revised the Church Order. For this reason it has become known as the Church Order of Dordrecht.

Since then the Reformed Churches in the Netherlands have maintained it — with an interruption between 1816 and 1834.

The churches of the Secession of 1834, at the instigation of the Rev. Hendrik de Cock, returned to this Church Order, as did the churches of the Doleantie of 1886 (the Second Secession).

Since the reunion of both groups in 1892, this Scriptural Order was maintained and strongly defended by Frederik L. Rutgers and Abraham Kuyper. However, since the twenties of this century a hierarchical interpretation and application became dominant, which led to a climax in the disruption of the unity of the churches by the general synods of the early forties.

The churches which liberated themselves from this yoke returned to the true interpretation of the Church Order's text.

The General Synod of Groningen-Zuid 1978 adopted the most recent revised version.

9. The Canadian Reformed Churches held their first General Synod — then called "National Synod" — at Carman in November, 1954. Article 73 of the Acts informs us that in a letter to the Dutch sister churches it was stated that the Canadian churches had adopted the Church Order of the churches in the Netherlands. However, they were aware of several difficulties. Therefore Synod "stated the necessity of revision of the Church Order with regard to the 'special Canadian situation' (Acts, Art. 94) and took decisions."

This is a quotation from the Acts of General Synod New Westminster 1971. These Acts contain a summary of the decisions taken by its predecessors. This summary goes on as follows:

   b. Synod 1958 dealt with proposals of revision regarding nineteen articles of the Church Order (See Acts, Art. 60, 61, 72).
   c. Synod 1968 discussed an overture of Regional Synod East, Sept. 1968, to appoint a Committee with the mandate: a general revision of the Church Order. The grounds for this overture ("without pretending to be exhaustive") were:
      1. several articles (five are mentioned) need *corrections*;
      2. several (ten are mentioned) "should be *changed*;"
      3. some (four are mentioned) "could be *dropped*;"
      4. *additions* might be advisable (seven were suggested).

This Synod decided to "continue the 'Committee on the Revision of the Church Order,' appointed by General Synod 1968," and "to give the following, more specific mandate to this Committee":

   a. to undertake a general revision of the . . . Church Order, as much as "the profit of the Churches demand it" (Art.86 C.O.), with preservation of the Reformed character of this Church Order; paying special attention to suggestions, submitted in the past by Churches and major assemblies concerning change, correction, updating and/or deletion of articles, as well as profitable additions.

At the General Synod Toronto 1974 there was a draft of 28 articles, wherefore this assembly decided "to continue the Committee on the Church Order to complete its mandate." The Committee was instructed "to seriously consider the report of the Dutch Committee ad hoc, received via the Committee on Correspondence with Churches Abroad, and the actions the Dutch Sister-Churches may take in this matter." It further adopted a new article regarding the Property of the Churches — in the present Church Order, Article 75.

Drafts of 33 and 22 articles respectively were presented to the General Synods of Coaldale 1977 and Smithville 1980. However, the continued Committee could be honourably discharged when the General Synod Cloverdale 1983 could decide (Acts, Art.91):

3. to adopt the revised Church Order (with some amendments);
4. to have the Revised Church Order published in the *Book of Praise*, and as a separate booklet for use in the Churches.

The General Synod Burlington-West 1986, finally, made some changes in Articles 13, 44, and 72 (Acts, Art. 94-5). This may explain the slight differences between the text as printed in this booklet and that in the 1984 edition of the *Book of Praise*.

10. Finally we would like to refer once again to the *Ordonnances Ecclésiastiques* of 1561. The men who compiled it and Geneva's consistory which adopted it, were convinced that it would become an important document in the life of the congregation. That is why its final article contained the following arrangement:

> From the year 1564 this Church Order shall be read publicly every three years in St. Peter's, on the first Sunday of the month of June.

The congregation had to become familiar with this document.

Our Church Order does not contain such a stipulation; yet we can fully agree with the committee of the Dutch churches which reported to their 1978 General Synod and wrote also these words (our translation):

> One thing has become clear during our work . . . the eminent significance of the knowledge concerning the Church Order for the peace, the edification, and the continuance of Reformed church life. Therefore it would be very useful if the Church Order were to be made accessible to office bearers as well as ordinary church members.

We may draw our readers' attention in particular to the word ''peace'' in this quotation. In I Corinthians 14: 32 the Apostle Paul states:

> God is not a God of confusion but of peace.

It is only then that he finishes this chapter by saying:

> All things should be done decently and in order.

Christ's church has to live by the peace of God which is in Him, the Saviour, and must thereto maintain order in her midst!

CHURCH ORDER

I. Introduction

ARTICLE 1. Purpose and Division

> *For the maintenance of good order in the Church of Christ it is necessary that there be: offices and supervision of doctrine; assemblies; worship, sacraments, and ceremonies; and discipline.*
>
> *These matters will be dealt with in the above-mentioned order.*

From our "Preliminary Remarks" (sub 1 and 10) we may repeat: This very first sentence of the Church Order refers to the apostolic command in I Corinthians 14:40: "All things should be done decently and in order."

Desiring to obey this command our churches have established a good order by adopting a number of regulations in respect of the four different matters that are mentioned in this initial article.

It contains more than just a formal division of the Church Order; it has a confessional character also. For it claims that according to Holy Scripture the offices, assemblies, supervision of doctrine, worship, and church discipline cannot be excluded from the churches of the Lord.

At this stage it is not necessary to give a summary of the various parts in Scripture informing us about God's will regarding these matters. That will be done when we begin to discuss them in sequential order. Besides, our confessional writings and the respective liturgical forms supply us with a sufficient number of prooftexts.

Our Church Order is based on "revealed principles" — see the Preliminary Remarks under 3.

These fundamentals, then, have been further worked out in view of our church life. This is why we will find all sorts of arrangements and agreements concerning the training for and the calling to the Ministry of the Word, consistory meetings, classes and synods, liturgical forms, congregational singing, the way in which church discipline is to be administered, etc.

By reason of the above, then, we can clearly see that this first article is indeed not just a summary of the contents and a formal division of our Church Order, although it definitely does offer such a formal division.

This is why after this introductory article, I. Article 1, we are going to deal with:

II. Articles 2-28, on the offices and supervision of doctrine.
III. Articles 29-51, on the assemblies.
IV. Articles 52-65, on worship, sacraments and ceremonies.
V. Articles 66-73, on Christian discipline.
Articles 74-76 are concluding articles.

II. Offices and Supervision of Doctrine

ARTICLE 2. The Offices

The offices are those of the minister of the Word, of the elder, and of the deacon.

In accordance with Holy Scripture the Church Order distinguishes three offices:

1. that of the minister of the Word.
   They are called:
   those who labour in preaching and teaching, I Timothy 5:17.
   (men who have) to give instruction in sound doctrine and also to confute those who contradict it, Titus 1:9.
2. that of elders.
   They are called:
   elders (presbyters), Acts 14:23; James 5:14.
   leaders, Hebrews 13:7, 17, 24.
   administrators, I Corinthians 12:28.
   bishops (episcopoi), Philippians 1:1; I Timothy 3:2; Titus 1:7.
   overseers (= bishops, episcopoi), Acts 20:28.
3. that of deacons.
   They are mentioned in Philippians 1:1; I Timothy 3:8, 10, 12, and without that name in Acts 6:1-7.

The first section of our Church Order deals with these respective offices.

We can make the following subdivision:

Article 3   : on the offices in general and the calling thereto.
Articles 4-18 : on the office of the ministers.
Articles 19-21: on the training for the Ministry.
Articles 22-25: on the office of the elders and the deacons.
Articles 26-28: on the offices and the Confession, false doctrine, and civil authorities.

As may be evident from this summary, most attention focuses on the ministers.

This does not contradict the contents of Article 80, but can simply be explained by the fact that they are full-time workers throughout their entire lives, so that certain regulations concerning them had to be established which do not apply to the elders and deacons.

Some of the ministers may receive a special calling, for Mission work — the task of missionaries being explained in Article 18 — or for the training of students in the Ministry of the Word — with which matter Article 19 will deal; John Calvin even considered the latter to hold a special office, that of the "doctors."

Our forms for the ordination of ministers, elders, and deacons, clearly confirm that they all are serving under Jesus Christ, the Head of the church.

18

The regulations and stipulations contained in our Church Order are very useful for the faithful execution of their respective offices in the service of the Lord who governs His church.

ARTICLE 3. The Calling to Office

No one shall take any office upon himself without having been lawfully called thereto.

Only those male members shall be eligible for office who have made profession of faith and may be considered to meet the conditions as set forth in Holy Scripture, e.g. in I Timothy 3 and Titus 1.

The election to any office shall take place with the cooperation of the congregation, after preceding prayers, and according to the regulations adopted for that purpose by the consistory with the deacons.

The consistory with the deacons shall be free to give the congregation the opportunity beforehand to draw the attention of the consistory to brothers deemed fit for the respective offices.

The consistory with the deacons shall present to the congregation either as many candidates as there are vacancies to be filled, or at the most twice as many, from which number the congregation shall choose as many as are needed.

Those elected shall be appointed by the consistory with the deacons in accordance with the adopted regulations.

Prior to the ordination or installation the names of the appointed brothers shall be publicly announced to the congregation for its approbation on at least two consecutive Sundays.

The ordination or installation shall take place with the use of the relevant forms.

The first sentence of this article is based on Scripture. Hebrews 5:4 says:

And one does not take the honour upon himself, but he is called by God, just as Aaron was.

The fact that this stipulation has been made is at the same time a consequence of the apostolic command issued in I Corinthians 14:40.

This is clearly stated in the Form for the Ordination of Elders (*Book of Praise*, 1984, p.630), where it says:

. . . being stewards of the house of God, they are to take care that in the congregation all things are done decently and in good order.

This article, then, is fundamental to the ensuing articles.

In the history of the Reformed churches there happened to be a clear reason for inserting an article like this in the Church Order.

During the days of the great Reformation all sorts of people presented themselves as "preachers:" ex-priests and ex-monks, who had been deposed or dismissed because of misbehaviour and who then sought to earn a living by acting as "travelling preachers." There were also the Anabaptists who claimed to have "the inner light," a special revelation, and consequently an "inward calling" to the Ministry.

As for the term "inward calling," it would be better to avoid it and to restrict the use of the word "calling" to the procedure described in this article.

Yet, those who would like to become a minister should — as H. Bouwman, *Gereformeerd Kerkrecht*, 1928, Volume I, pp.368-70, writes — possess:

1. A persistent love for the gospel ministry, a strong desire to serve God and His kingdom in the ministry, born of prayerful meditation. 2. A certain amount of ability. He who aspires to the ministry must not only have the necessary strength of body and character, but also certain indispensable talents, as, for instance, pertaining to mind and speech. 3. Readiness to deny oneself utterly; readiness to serve the Lord wherever and however He may appoint. 4. Unselfish aims; a desire to see God glorified and His kingdom extended. None should desire the ministry merely as a profession and as a livelihood. 5. An open road; the ways and means essential for the necessary preparation will be provided by God in His providence, if one is truly called of Him. If one feels called to the ministry but finds that the road leading to the ministry is providentially closed, all his prayers notwithstanding, then he may be sure that he is not actually called of God" (translated in I. Van Dellen and M. Monsma, *The Revised Church Order Commentary*, 1969, p.30).

While older versions of the Church Order first of all contained a number of articles regarding the ministers of the Word, this present Order starts with an article on the calling to any of the three offices mentioned in Article 2.

In the past a number of churches had some special regulations for the calling of a minister, while others had to improvise on such an occasion. This revised Church Order promotes the adoption of regulations which can be used for the election to any office.

True Reformed churches cannot comply with today's trend to open the offices to female members. This article, therefore, rules that only male members shall be eligible for office. Besides, they must be "confessing members" and meet the Scriptural conditions set forth in I Timothy 3 and Titus 1.

Then, the actual procedure is described.

First of all the article states that the election to any office shall take place with the cooperation of the congregation. The churches are on their guard against any form of hierarchy, "consistoriocracy" included.

This cooperation is in accordance with Holy Scripture: Acts 6:3 and II Corinthians 8:19.

The election shall be preceded by prayers. It will not be necessary to emphasize that the invocation of the Lord is an essential element in the election.

This suggests a formal meeting of the congregation, convened for this particular purpose.

The Church Order is silent on the question whether or not the female members are entitled to participate in the election of office-bearers — here and there "a lance is being broken" for the female communicant members to be given the right to cast their vote.

However, it may be clear that every member of the congregation has the right to attend and follow the procedure with interest, taking part in the preceding prayers.

Some emphasis is put on the necessity of having a set of regulations.

One of the rules in many of them is that the members of the congregation have the opportunity to cooperate in the very first stages of the election of elders and deacons, even of the calling of a minister, by bringing to the attention of the consistory names of persons whom they consider suitable. However, the Church Order does not make this compulsory. It only says that the consistory "shall be free" to give this opportunity beforehand.

As for the presentation made by the consistory to the congregation, it is remarkable that the first possibility mentioned is that of a "single nomination." This may be explained from the fact that Article 3 is intended to cover the calling to any office, that of the ministry of the Word included. For the days of presenting a "double number" or even more names for the calling of a minister are over!

However, the usual way of electing elders and deacons is that of presenting double the required number, from which the enfranchised members can make their choice. In exceptional cases, e.g. when an insufficient number of candidates is available, a "single" presentation can be made.

It may be clear from the text of this article that, after the enfranchised members of the congregation have elected as many candidates as are needed, the actual appointment — or, in case of a minister, the calling — is done by the consistory.

This article, correctly, puts the approval of the congregation after the appointment of the elected brothers by the consistory (with the deacons, as the text says; but we will not time and again repeat this). The presentation of double the required number is not to be approved by the congregation. This would create unnecessary problems.

21

Relevant rules for the ordination or installation have been adopted by the churches. Their text has been published e.g. in the *Book of Praise.*

Most congregations — if not all — have a set of regulations including all the elements mentioned in this article.

They may even contain rules for the preparation of double the required number at the consistory meeting — or otherwise the consistory may have adopted some separate rules for this purpose.

The normal procedure is that the names of all brothers brought to the attention of the consistory are put on two separate lists, one for the elders, and one for the deacons; that the members of the consistory and the deacons can add other names to these lists; that each name is briefly discussed, the point of discussion being the persons ability to serve in the office of elder or deacon; that names are taken from these lists by common consent only; and that double the required number is arrived at by the outcome of a secret ballot.

It is not exclusively up to the person appointed to the office of elder or deacon to decide whether or not he can accept. If for some reason a brother requests to be relieved, the consistory must examine the situation, and — if the reason is found to be valid — can then relieve him of this calling.

As for the calling of a minister, in the century of the Reformation the election of a minister of the Word was entrusted to the elders only. Later on the deacons were also involved, the number of people who were responsible in this respect being in that way increased. However, for approximately the last one hundred years, it has been the general practice to let the members of the congregation cooperate.

It seems to be wise to organize a secret ballot — a simple "yes" or "no" vote — for the calling of a minister.

It may be interesting to hear about the tradition maintained in the congregation of Dutch refugees in London (from 1550) — called by Festus Hommius "the mother of the Dutch churches." Only the male members of 21 years and over were entitled to participate in the election — public profession of faith was made at the early age of 14! A special day of fasting and prayer was organized, with two church services during which the significance of the offices was explained. During the following days the members could hand in their ballot papers. A consistory meeting was then convened, during which the elected brothers were appointed. They were summoned to the meeting and personally instructed on the significance of their offices, after which they were asked whether they could accept their appointment. On the next Sunday an announcement was made in order to obtain the silent approval of the congregation.

Another peculiarity in the London congregation was that the laying on of hands was not restricted to the ministers, but that it was applied to all office-bearers.

We should realize that (as the old Form for the Ordination of Elders, in the *Book of Praise*, 1972, p.533, said), "The offices always are to remain distinct one from the other." A minister has not been called to the office of a deacon, a deacon not to that of an elder, and an elder not to the office of a deacon or of a minister.

We can say that these three distinct offices were originally united in that of the apostles, but it is not for nothing that shortly after Pentecost — and certainly when the temporary office of the "apostolate" was about to be terminated — a development took place leading to the institution of three distinct offices.

One of the consequences of the three offices being distinct is, that "reading services" should not too easily replace "preaching services."

It is not correct to say that in these "reading services" the Word of God is not heard, but the official administration and distribution of God's Word is entrusted to those who, by means of the execution of this particular office, according to the apostolic command, have been called thereto.

The "laying on" of the final Benediction has been entrusted to the ministers only. The reason for this is that it is considered as a sort of summary of the "official" administration of God's Word by the bearer of the office of minister of the Word.

In some sister churches — in particular those in the Netherlands — voices are heard which plead for granting permission to the "reading elder" to do the same. A possible solution to this "problem" may be that the elder uses the same formula as the minister — so not changing the word "you" into "us" — but without raising his hands, so that it all sounds as a sort of prayer.

The same can be said about the Salutation at the beginning of the services, in view of the fact that this has more the character of a Christian greeting.

All that is stated in this Article is a further elaboration on what we confess in our Belgic Confession of Faith, Article 31, which says:

> We believe that ministers of God's Word, the elders and the deacons ought to be chosen to their offices by lawful election of the Church, with prayer and in good order, as stipulated by the Word of God. Therefore everyone shall take care not to intrude by improper means. He shall wait for the time that he is called by God so that he may have sure testimony and thus be certain that his call comes from the Lord.

The concept conveyed in the last line is also expressed in the first question of the Form for Ordination of ministers of the Word of God and that of elders and deacons (in the *Book of Praise*, 1984, pp. 621, 626, and 632):

> Do you feel in your heart that God Himself through His congregation has called you to this holy ministry? (to these offices?)

ARTICLE 4. Eligibility for the Ministry

    A. ELIGIBILITY

      Only those shall be called to the office of minister of the Word who
1. *Have been declared eligible for call by the Churches;*
2. *Are already serving in that capacity in one of the Churches; or*
3. *Have been declared eligible in, or are serving in one of the Churches with which the Canadian Reformed Churches maintain a sister-Church relationship.*

    B. DECLARED ELIGIBLE

      Only those shall be declared eligible for call within the Churches who
1. *Have passed a preparatory examination by the classis in which they live. This examination shall not take place unless those presenting themselves for it submit the documents necessary to prove that they are members in good standing of one of the Churches and have successfully completed a course of study as required by the Churches.*
2. *Served in the Churches with which the Canadian Reformed Churches do not maintain a sister-Church relationship, and have been examined by the classis in which they live, with due observance of the general ecclesiastical regulations adopted for that purpose.*
3. *Have been examined according to the rule described in Article 8.*

    C. CALLING TWICE

      For a second call to the same minister in the same vacancy the approval of classis shall be required.

    D. COUNSELLOR

      When a vacant Church extends a call, the advice of the counsellor shall be asked.

As for the matter of the eligibility for the Ministry and the ordination or installation of ministers of the Word, the revised Church Order is clearer than the old version. The latter, in one single article, dealt with the preparatory examination as well as the peremptory examination, which could easily lead to confusion. The new version discusses the preparatory examination in Article 4, while Article 5 deals with the peremptory (i.e. deciding) examination.

That one must be declared eligible for call by the churches — as will be described under B — is a further elaboration on what is stated in the first sentence of Article 3: "No one shall take any office upon himself without having been lawfully called thereto."

That those who are already serving as ministers of the Word in one of the churches are eligible seems to be a matter of course. However, there is a sort of silent "gentlemen's agreement" that, very peculiar circumstances excepted, a minister is not called by another congregation unless he has served his present congregation for a number of years — say, three or four years.

As for A 3, before this was included in the Church Order there happened to be some uncertainty and even confusion regarding the eligibility of candidates to the ministry who had been declared eligible for a call in sister churches. Since international contacts are now more intensely maintained, it was wise to include in our Church Order a regulation on this matter.

Article 5 C will deal with a colloquium with ministers who, while serving in a sister church, have been called to one of the churches in the federation of the Canadian Reformed Churches.

Those who have not served in a sister church will have to meet the requirements mentioned in Article 5 A.

As for those who can be declared eligible, three different groups are summed up.

The first one is a group of persons who "have successfully completed a course of study as required by the Churches." For this end the churches maintain their own Theological College at Hamilton, Ontario.

These people have to undergo a preparatory examination by the classis in which they live.

This examination consists of the following parts:
1. a conversation between a number of delegates appointed by the classis for this purpose and the candidate on the motives of the latter that have led him to seek admission to the Ministry of the Word; and the acceptance of their report by the classis.
2. the delivering of a draft sermon on a prescribed text from Scripture. The candidate is informed about this text three weeks prior to the exam.
    Copies of the draft sermon are to be sent to the examiners appointed for this purpose one week before the day of the examination.
3. an examination in the knowledge of Holy Scripture.
4. an examination in the candidate's ability regarding the exegesis of the Old Testament.
5. the same regarding the exegesis of the New Testament. At least two weeks prior to the examination the examiners concerned shall assign the chapters from the Scripture on which he will be examined, one from the Old Testament and one from the New Testament.
6. an examination in the doctrine of the churches.

In addition to achieving favourable result in all this, the candidate must formally subscribe to the Three Forms of Unity; he is then declared as being eligible to be called by one of our churches. Normally he is entitled to speak an edifying word for a period of twelve months.

It may be superfluous to mention that, prior to this preparatory exam, the candidate must be able to show a declaration of membership in full rights. Such a declaration should be issued by the consistory of the congregation to which he belonged during the last twelve months or more. It goes without saying, however, that in the first place he must be able to furnish proof of having successfully completed his final examinations at the theological college.

As for B 2, a minister who, e.g., has left a church that has become apostate, and after having joined one of our churches would like to serve as a minister within our churches, has to be examined by the classis in which he lives. This examination must be undertaken ''with due observance of the general ecclesiastical regulations adopted for that purpose.'' These regulations were adopted by General Synod Edmonton 1965 (Acts Articles 39 and 46). They are:

A. With respect to those who are serving or have served in Churches with which the Canadian Reformed Churches do not maintain church-correspondence:
  1. they shall not be called unless they have been declared eligible for a call in the Churches;
  2. they may be declared eligible for a call only after
    a. they have submitted proof of their ordination as a minister;
    b. they have submitted a written exposition of the reasons why they desire to be declared eligible for call within the Churches;
    c. they submit a good testimony about their conduct;
    d. they submit themselves to an examination on the level of the preparatory and peremptory examinations.
  The Classis of their domicile shall examine them in the presence and with concurring advice of the Deputies of the Particular Synod, ad art.49 C.O.
B. With respect to those who are serving or have served in Churches with which the Canadian Reformed Churches maintain Church-correspondence:
  1. they may be called without first having been declared eligible for call in the Churches;
  2. they may be admitted to the ministry in the Churches if they
    a. submit to the Classis that is asked to approve the call
      1. proof of their ordination,
      2. proof that they have been called by one of the Churches,
      3. a statement that they wish to accept this call,
      4. a testimony about their doctrine and life,
      5. proof that they were duly released from their former charge;
    b. submit themselves to a colloquium doctum which will deal especially with the Reformed doctrine and church polity.

The General Synod Orangeville 1968 deleted the word d
in *Colloquium doctum* (Acts Article 109).

Article 8 will separately deal with persons of exceptional gifts. After the completion of the procedure described in that article, they are declared eligible for the Ministry.

There is also a rule for the repeated calling of the same minister in the same vacancy. Such a call requires the approval of classis. The reason for a repeated call is usually the fact that since the first call was declined there has been a change in the circumstances, either on the side of the minister or on that of the calling congregation. The renewed contact between the church and the minister concerned leads, as a rule, to the immediate acceptance of the call; in all this — as a matter of course — what has been stipulated in Article 9 is honoured.

That in such a case the classis is involved must be considered in the light of the "theme" of the Church Order, that "all things should be done decently and in order."

Article 45 will deal with the position of a counsellor. His advice shall be asked when a vacant church extends a call. This does not necessarily mean that his opinion must be sought regarding the candidate or minister to be called — although this would indeed be a wise thing to do. His only duty is to see to it that the calling takes place in "good order." Even in this respect the churches want to obey the apostolic command of I Corinthians 14:40!

ARTICLE 5. Ordination and Installation of Ministers of the Word

> *A. Regarding those who have not served in the ministry before, the following shall be observed:*
>
> *1. They shall be ordained only after classis has approved the call. Classis shall approve the call*
> *a. Upon satisfactory testimony concerning the soundness of doctrine and conduct of the candidate, signed by the consistory of the Church to which he belongs;*
> *b. Upon a peremptory examination of the candidate by classis with satisfactory results. This examination shall take place with the cooperation and concurring advice of deputies of the regional synod.*
>
> *2. For the ordination they shall show also to the consistory good testimonials concerning their doctrine and conduct from the Church(es) to which they have belonged since their preparatory examination.*
>
> *B. Regarding those who are serving in the ministry the following shall be observed:*
> *They shall be installed after classis has approved the call.*
> *For this approbation as well as for the installation the minister shall show good testimonials concerning his*

doctrine and conduct, together with a declaration from the consistory with the deacons and from classis that he has been honourably discharged from his service in that Church and classis, or from the Church only, in case he remains within the same classis.

C. *For the classical approbation of a call of those who are serving in one of the Churches with which the Canadian Reformed Churches maintain a sister-Church relationship a colloquium shall be required which will deal especially with the doctrine and polity of the Canadian Reformed Churches.*

D. *For the classical approbation of a call shall further be required a declaration by the calling Church that the proper announcements have been made and that the congregation has given its approval to the call.*

Each of the four sections of this article deals with the classical approval of calls.

Re A:

The first section regards "those who have not served in the ministry before," i.e., so "candidates" and "octavists" (as people are called who, according to Article 8, have been endowed with exceptional gifts).

Two conditions must be met before approval can be granted by the classis to which the calling church belongs.

a. The consistory of the congregation of which he who is called is a member must declare that he is sound in doctrine and conduct, which declaration must be handed over to the classis.

b. The candidate must pass the so-called peremptory (decisive) exam.

Deputies of the regional synod must attend; their advice must concur with the classical judgment. The reason for this may be clear: the ordination of a candidate has consequences as far as the federation of churches is concerned, as may become evident in some of the following articles (e.g. Articles 9 and 15).

This peremptory examination is much longer and more intense than the preparatory exam.

As in the case of the latter, this exam also should not bear an exclusively "scientific" character — which does happen in the case of the final examinations at the Theological College, although it must become clear e.g. that the candidate is able to read the Bible in its original languages. These two ecclesiastical examinations are intended to convince the churches, via their delegates, that the candidate is able to serve the congregation that has called him in all the various aspects of the Ministry of the Word.

For this reason he is examined:

1. in his ability to deliver a sermon (the text is to be chosen by himself; the draft is to be sent in one week prior to the examination).

And further in the following subjects:

2. the knowledge of Holy Scripture.
3. the exegesis of the Old Testament.
4. the exegesis of the New Testament (at least three weeks before the peremptory examination the candidate is informed about the two chapters from the Old Testament and the two chapters from the New Testament in which he will be examined).
5. the doctrine of the churches.
6. his knowledge of the contents of our creeds and confessions.
7. ethics.
8. church history.
9. church politics.
10. the ''pastoral subjects:''
    a. homiletics, the ''art'' of preparing sermons.
    b. liturgics.
    c. catechetics.
    d. poimenics, pastoral care during visits, etc.
    e. diaconics.

Here again certain documents have to be tabled first:

a. the letter of call.
b. a declaration of acceptance of the call.
c. a declaration regarding the candidate's eligibility to be called as a minister, issued by the classis that has examined him preparatorily.
d. once again: a declaration, issued by the church to which he belonged since his preparatory examination, that he is a member in full rights.

If the result of the examination is positive, the candidate must sign the Subscription Form for Ministers of the Word.

From the classis he receives a certificate designating him as being admitted to the Ministry of the Word.

This way the classis grants its approval of the call extended to the candidate.

As for another condition to be met by the calling church, see under D.

What if the candidate in the opinion of the classis and the deputies fails to pass? (Considering the level of the training at the colleges of our own churches and our sister churches, this is not very likely, and would be an exception!) Then the candidate may come to the conclusion that it is not God's will that he enter the Ministry of the Word. The calling church may also withdraw its call. However, if both parties desire this, a re-examination at a later date may be requested and granted. Obviously such a re-examination should not be granted if the candidate has not been found to be sound in faith or conduct.

A second regulation does not regard the classical approval but the ordination. It says that before this ordination takes place the candidate must show to the consistory a good testimonial concerning his doctrine and conduct from the church or churches of which he was a member since his preparatory examination.

This is another safeguard for the church concerned.

That the ordination must take place in a church service may follow from the last line of Article 3, which says that "The ordination or installation shall take place with the use of the relevant forms." It is the public effectuation and acceptance of the extended call.

This is emphasized by the contents of the form adopted for this purpose, for it contains valuable instruction for the congregation and the person concerned. It says:

Let us first hear what Holy Scripture teaches about the office of ministers of the Word.

It further contains the stipulation that the candidate, among other things, publicly promise

faithfully to discharge the duties of (his) office and to adorn the doctrine of God with a godly life.

Then the actual ordination follows, in which the officiating minister shall lay his hands upon the head of the ordinee.

After a brief exhortation to both the newly ordained minister and the congregation, the ceremony is concluded with a public prayer.

We just mentioned the Laying on of Hands.

Although the Church Order is silent on this, it is a special part of the ordination ceremony.

It shall not take place in an installation ceremony. In the *Book of Praise*, 1984, p. 623 and also p. 628, the following is stated: "The laying on of hands shall not take place in the case of those who are already in the ministry."

The church of Rome, the high church party in the Anglican church, and various other churches believe that there has to be an uninterrupted chain of ordinations, conducted by bishops who in turn were themselves ordained by bishops, and that this chain has to reach back to the apostles, whose successors the ordinees claim to be. The above-mentioned public prayer however clearly shows us that imposition does not mean a transfer of office; it is mainly a prayer for the gift of the Holy Spirit.

It reads:

We pray Thee, wilt Thou by Thy Spirit equip him to the ministry to which Thou hast called him.

As far as this is concerned, our ordination ceremony runs

parallel to that of the Presbyterian churches. In their "Form of Church-Government" we find the following section on the ordination:

. . . the presbytery, or the ministers sent from them for ordination, shall solemnly set him apart to the office and work of the ministry, by laying their hands on him, which is to be accompanied with a short prayer of blessing, to this effect: "Thankfully acknowledging the great mercy of God in sending Jesus Christ for the redemption of his people; and for his ascension to the right hand of God the Father, and thence pouring out his Spirit, and giving gifts to men, apostles, evangelists, prophets, pastors, and teachers; for the gathering and building up of his church, and for fitting and inclining this man to this great work; to entreat him to fit him with his Holy Spirit, to give him (who in his name we thus set apart to this holy service) to fulfil the work of his ministry in all things, that he may both save himself, and his people committed to his charge."

As soon as the LORD is asked "to fit him with His Holy Spirit," the imposition of hands must take place, for this form has here a note that says: "Here let them impose hands on his head."

The imposition ceremony means that the time and talents of the person concerned are no longer his alone but that he has been fully dedicated to the service of the LORD and must employ these talents and his time accordingly.

This is in full harmony with the character of the imposition of hands on Joshua and others (Numbers 28:18; I Timothy 4:14; 5:22; II Timothy 1:6).

This is also the reason why such a ceremony takes place only when a candidate is ordained, and not when a minister is installed in a new congregation.

There is certainly no apostolic command to this effect. In the past it was left to the churches' own discretion whether or not they would administer imposition. There was some concern regarding the possibility that the Roman Catholic view would take hold in our churches, as if in a certain magic or mystical way the necessary ability to discharge the duties of the office would be given by the imposition of hands. The Reformed churches preferred to keep at a safe distance from the Roman Catholic sacrament of the ordination into the priesthood.

Not so long ago it was a custom to invite all the ministers attending the ordination service to participate in the imposition ceremony. Our Church Order and the Ordination Form are silent about this. The Church Order of the Dutch and the Australian sister churches allow only the officiating minister to administer the imposition. This may be a matter of avoiding a "show."

But it could also be a first step towards the introduction of the laying on of hands at the ordination of elders and deacons — which is propagated by some. The question is raised: Why this difference in action at the respective ordinations; is this only because a minister is "full-time?" Is this in full accordance with Article 74 of the Church Order?

Further we would like to draw the attention to the fact that our Church Order does not make mention of an "inaugural sermon," let alone of a rule in this respect.

We would not like to say that this tradition must be abolished, as long as we do not expect the sermon to contain a program of proposed action. The minister concerned just begins his work in the congregation when he delivers his first sermon. Speeches of welcome can damage the character of the church service, and are better left to be delivered at a special congregational meeting.

Re B:

Classis has also to approve the call extended to someone who is already serving in the ministry.

Apart from the "good testimonies concerning his doctrine and conduct," a declaration must be tabled regarding his discharge from the service of his previous church and the classis to which this church belongs.

As a matter of course, a declaration from the classis is not needed when the calling church is located in the same classis, because the minister concerned is not "honourably discharged from his service" in that classis. This may be worth mentioning because our classes cover large territories.

Re C:

Even in a situation wherein most of the ministers of our churches had their training for the Ministry at our own Theological College at Hamilton, it may happen that every now and then a minister is called who is serving a foreign sister church. Although such a minister has already passed the examinations mentioned in Articles 4 and 5, the churches deemed it wise to require a "colloquium," a discussion especially on doctrine and church polity which must make it clear that he really is a Reformed minister.

The same testimonials and declaration mentioned under B must be shown before the classis will be able to approve the call extended to such a minister.

Re D:

In each of the above mentioned cases the consistory of the church in question must announce the aspiring minister's name on two consecutive Sundays during the church service. In this way the — silent — approval of the congregation is obtained.

Lawful objections could be raised against the candidate's or the minister's doctrine, conduct, or his ability to serve as a minister.

In the event of difficulties proving to be insurmountable, the bond of churches must intervene, if need be, by dealing with an appeal.

This action from the side of the congregation is not only a matter of supervision over a future member but it is of great importance for the well-being of the congregation as the work of a minister of the Word is of great importance in the life of the congregation.

We would like to make a few brief remarks in conclusion.

First of all: Although under A and C some emphasis is put on the examination and the colloquium, we should not forget that the classical approval has to be obtained by the church extending the call — in which, as a matter of course, the cooperation of the candidate or minister concerned is required.

Further, we would like to point to the fact that a General Synod of the Dutch sister churches, that of Dordrecht 1893, decided that the approval of classis shall include its being satisfied that the calling church is in a position to provide adequate financial support for the minister, in accordance with Holy Scripture. It would be wise for our churches to follow this rule.

The same can be said regarding a rule made by the Synod Arnhem, 1902, that in the "letter of call" the financial support in case of retirement (superannuation) is to be included.

ARTICLE 6. Bound to a Church

> *No one shall serve in the ministry unless he is bound to a certain Church, to be stationed in a certain place, or to be sent out for the gathering of the Church from among the heathen or from among those who have become estranged from the gospel; or is to be charged with some other special ministerial task.*

Even historically this article follows the preceding ones. Originally it was inserted into the Church Order with the aim to stop the practice of the so-called "loose ministers." These were people who claimed to be on a level with the apostles and evangelists. They went from one place to another and preached wherever they could. However, this practice ceased as soon as the Reformed churches on the European continent became well established.

Meanwhile this article contains a principle of great significance. It is again of a confessional character.

The church of Rome claims: Wherever the priest is, there is the church. Other churches state: Every minister is a minister of the whole of the national church. But our Church Order takes the Scriptural stand. Holy Scripture presents to us "the angels of the seven churches," "the angel of the church in Ephesus," "the angel of the church in Smyrna," etc. (Revelation 1:20; 2:1, 8, 12, 18, 3:1, 7, 14).

This article, then, indicates the significant position of the local church.

Certainly, the church of the Lord Jesus Christ is a catholic and universal church. It is spread and dispersed over the entire world (Belgic Confession of Faith, Article 27). However,

> all and everyone are obliged to join it and unite with it, maintaining the unity of the Church. They must submit themselves to its instruction and discipline.

This means that they have

> to join this assembly wherever God has established it.

Well, this "congregation," this "doctrine and discipline" is to be found in the local church!

Consequently, as for the ministers of the Word, they have to preach the said doctrine and administer the above mentioned "discipline" in a local church, "their" church. They have to be bound to a certain church.

Are they allowed to preach in their sister churches? Article 10 will make it clear that this can only happen at the invitation and with the permission of the consistories concerned.

We, as Reformed churches, do not have any "ministers-in-general-service."

This function has been created by churches that cannot be called, or can no longer be called, "Reformed," because they are taking the above-mentioned course of the church of Rome.

Even our professors at the Theological College are not "ministers-in-general-service," but they are and remain ministers of a local church, having been "set apart for the training of students in the Ministry of the Word."

Concerning our missionaries, *mutatis mutandis*, the same thing can be said (Article 2).

This simple article, then, contains a fundamental principle of our Reformed church government!

All this is not contradicted by what follows after "unless he is bound to a certain Church, to be stationed in a certain place."

For even when a minister is "sent out for the gathering of the Church from among the heathen," etc., he is bound to a certain church. This church, then, sent him out. When he is "charged with some other special ministerial task," such as that of an army or hospital minister, he is charged by (again) "a certain Church."

This article in the meantime provides us with a Scriptural definition of mission work: it is a matter of "gathering the Church from among the heathen."

These days the borderline between "mission work" and "evangelizing" is very unclear. This may be the reason why it is added: "or from among those who have become estranged from the gospel." Of course, this does not cover all the activities of what is usually called "evangelism:" here the possibility is mentioned that a minister is set apart and sent out for this special task. But again we must give good attention to the formulation: This task is also one of "gathering the Church" from among these people — which does not necessarily mean that whenever and wherever possible a congregation must be instituted from among the converts, but that they must be called back to the church of the Lord Jesus Christ.

Mission work and evangelizing is not just a matter of trying to "save souls," but also a matter of church-gathering!

ARTICLE 7. Recent Converts

> *No one who has recently come to the confession of the Reformed Religion shall be declared eligible for call within the Churches unless he has been well tested for a reasonable period of time and has been carefully examined by classis with the cooperation of the deputies of the regional synod.*

This article speaks for itself. No further comment is needed, in our opinion.

It shows again the care of the churches for the faithful preaching of God's Word.

But at the same time it proves that the door is open to those who really want to minister in a true church of the Lord Jesus Christ.

They, too, are acknowledged as gifts from the glorified Saviour (Ephesians 4:11).

ARTICLE 8. Exceptional Gifts

> *Persons who have not pursued the regular course of study shall not be admitted to the ministry unless there is assurance of their exceptional gifts of godliness, humility, modesty, good intellect, and discretion, as well as the gift of public speech.*
> *When such persons present themselves for the ministry, classis, after the approval of regional synod, shall examine them in a preparatory examination and allow them to speak an edifying word in the Churches of the classis; and further deal with them as it shall deem edifying, with observance of the general ecclesiastical regulations adopted for this purpose.*

This article states that the rule is: No admission to the Ministry of God's Word without a theological training, but it does stipulate a course of action in the case of an exception. There may be persons with exceptional gifts.

These gifts — which are also required from those who have followed a theological training — must be convincingly evident as being exceptional.

Not for nothing is godliness mentioned as the first of these gifts. The person concerned must be filled with the Holy Spirit and the fear of the LORD.

Humility is the second one — his exceptional gifts could easily make him proud and full of conceit. However, his godliness has to be proved in his humility.

Modesty means that he leads a quiet and unblameable life.

One of the gifts must also be an exceptionally good intellect: he must have an understanding of Scripture and be able to explain it to others.

Discretion means that he must be able to distinguish between sound doctrine and heresy, and have a certain amount of insight into human character.

Apart from all this he should possess the gift of public speech, so that he will be able to express himself in a clear way.

When such a person presents himself for admission to the Ministry in this extraordinary way, the classis shall examine him, upon the approval of the regional synod.

This means that the local consistory and the classis to which his congregation belongs have to be convinced that he possesses all of these exceptional gifts. When that has been achieved, each will present a certificate to the regional synod, concerning these gifts. Investigations having been made and the regional synod having been sufficiently assured as to the truth of these testimonies, approval is granted, and the classis will then subject the person in question to a preparatory examination.

This examination is identical to the one mentioned in Article 5, with the exception that the knowledge of ancient languages is not essential.

If the examination has a favourable result, the classis grants him permission to speak an edifying word in the churches of the classis for a certain period of time. In this way he has the opportunity to practise. This happens under supervision of the consistories of the classis-churches, while the "sermons" are usually examined by some of the ministers appointed by the classis for this purpose.

When it becomes apparent that this also has favourable results, the classis declares him eligible to be called to the Ministry of the Word.

All this is included in the "general regulations" mentioned in the final sentence of this article.

It may be clear that the churches want to be diligent in caring for the faithful preaching of God's Word in the church of the Lord Jesus Christ.

ARTICLE 9. From One Church to Another

A minister, once lawfully called, shall not leave the Church to which he is bound to take up the ministry elsewhere without the consent of the consistory with the deacons and the approval of classis.

36

On the other hand, no Church shall receive him unless he has presented a proper certificate of release from the Church and the classis where he served, or of the Church only, if he remains within the same classis.

This article has been set in the negative: "a minister shall not . . .," and "no Church shall . . . ." This is based on the words "once lawfully called." We find them also in Article 12, where they are explained by their context: a minister is "bound to the service of the Church for life."

As soon as another church has extended a call to a minister, he must decide between two callings: either to stay in his present congregation or to accept the call extended to him by that other church.

However, as for the latter, the consent is required of the body that was involved in his former call, the consistory with the deacons, as is also the approval of classis.

A subsequent regulation regards the church that extended the call: this church shall not receive him unless he presents a proper certificate of release from the church and the classis where he served — except if he remains within the same classis (see at Article 5B).

This is another rule that has been adopted in order to obey the apostolic command: "All things should be done decently and in order."

It is intended to prevent malpractices and frictions between the churches concerned.

As for the procedure of extending a call, we may refer to our comment on Articles 3 and 4. For the installation, see at Article 5B.

ARTICLE 10. Proper Support

The consistory with the deacons, as representing the congregation, shall be bound to provide for the proper support of its minister(s).

Scripture teaches that "the labourer deserves his wages" (Luke 10:5; Matthew 10:10).

The ministers of the Word must be maintained by those among whom they are working. "The Lord commanded that those who proclaim the gospel should get their living by the gospel (I Corinthians 9:14; cf. Galatians 6:6).

This duty of the congregation is executed by the consistory that represents the congregation.

According to Articles 5 and 6, the counsellor's advice must be sought in the case of a vacant congregation extending a call to a candidate or a minister. The reason for this is that even this "shall be done decently and in good order."

A consequence of this is that the counsellor sees to it that the financial support which is promised in the "letter of call" is sufficient indeed.

Apart from this, the accepted call must have the approval of the classis. Then the "letter of call" shall be tabled, allowing the classis to assure itself as to the adequacy of the honorarium.

All this is a matter of brotherly supervision for the well-being of the churches.

A minister must be able to discharge the duties of his office without any financial worries.

This article does not give any directions regarding the way in which the money shall be raised. The best way, in our opinion, is that of voluntary but regular contributions.

The provisions of some directives is not in conflict with the voluntary character of these contributions.

The addition of "collections for the church" should be avoided.

The best way to deal with the financial affairs of the church is to include in the annual budget the whole of the expenditure: also the quota for the training for the Ministry, for Mission work, etc., so that the weekly collections can be restricted to charity, not only as far as the indigent in the own congregation are concerned but also covering all sorts of needs in God's wide world. This may give the weekly collections in the church services more the character of an offer of thanksgiving, and will prevent them from becoming a matter of routine. It brings them in line with the origin of church "collections," a reflection of which we find in Lord's Day 38 of our Catechism where it says that we must "diligently attend the church of God, to hear God's Word, to use the sacraments, to call publicly upon the LORD, and to give Christian offerings for the poor." In the ancient Christian church the celebration was often combined with a so-called *agapè*, a love-meal; in which the richer members brought their own food and drink to church, part of which was used for the celebration of the Lord's Supper while what was left over was for a common meal in which also the needy participated (this is the background of what we read in I Corinthians 11:21). In the days of the Great Reformation it was again strongly emphasized: We shall celebrate the Lord's Supper together with the needy brothers and sisters, and the giving of alms shall be included in the liturgy of the Lord's Table. Only later on these offerings were separated from the administration of this sacrament, while initially the purpose remained the same: charity. Still later collections for other purposes were introduced.

It may occur that a congregation is unable fully to support a minister. Since it is very important that whenever and wherever possible every congregation has its own minister, the sister churches shall in such cases assist her. This shall be done through the classis, and if necessary through the regional synod.

ARTICLE 11. Dismissal

If a minister of the Word is judged unfit and incapable of serving the congregation fruitfully and to its edification, without there being any reason for Church discipline, the consistory with the deacons shall not dismiss him from his service within the congregation without the approbation of classis and the concurring advice of the deputies of regional synod, and not without proper arrangements regarding the support of the minister and his family for a reasonable period of time.

If no call is forthcoming in three years, he shall be declared released from his ministerial status by the classis in which he served last.

The admission to the Ministry of the Word takes place with the assistance and supervision of the classis and the deputies of the synod as representatives of the federation of churches.

The release and the dismissal are to take place in the same way. This applies to the following cases:

1. when a minister is going to retire according to Article 13.
2. when a minister for reasons of health can no longer remain in the place where he is serving but would quite well be able to serve a congregation in an entirely different environment.
3. when a minister does not have the talents to serve a congregation any longer than for a limited number of years.
4. when there are difficulties between the minister and his congregation and he would no longer be able to serve her fruitfully, and it is desirable that he be dissociated from his congregation.

It may be clear that in the cases 2-4 no sin punishable with suspension or deposition is involved.

Article 13 deals with case No. 1; Article 14 with the second case. No regulation has been included in our Church Order for what is mentioned under No. 3.

Article 11 deals with the last mentioned possibility.

It may be clear that in such a case an agreement must be made concerning financial support for the period of time during which the minister is not yet installed in another congregation — for he will be eligible for call during a period of three years — or has not embarked upon another profession.

If he is not called within that period of time, the classis in which he served last will release him from his ministerial status.

ARTICLE 12. Bound for Life

Inasmuch as a minister of the Word, once lawfully called, is bound to the service of the Church for life, he is not allowed to enter upon another vocation unless it be for exceptional and substantial reasons, of which the consistory with the deacons shall judge, and which shall receive the approval of classis with the concurring advice of deputies of regional synod.

Ministers are human, and they may be tempted to resign their office when instances of extreme difficulties could affect their health; when they could obtain a more lucrative position in society; or even when they would like to avoid church discipline.

However, our Church Order makes provision for other possibilities. A minister of the Word could, e.g., be appointed to an important political function in which he would be able to contribute considerably to the well-being of the country. He could also be appointed as a professor at a university or college.

This, however, is not his own decision only. The consistory and the classis, together with the deputies of the regional synod — the same bodies which had their share in his admission to the ministry — have to see to it that there are indeed substantial reasons for him to enter upon another vocation. In such cases the person concerned no longer has the right to call himself a minister.

ARTICLE 13. Retirement of Ministers

If a minister is rendered incapable of performing the duties of his office because of age, illness, or physical or mental disability, he shall retain the honour and title of minister of the Word. He shall also retain his official bond with the Church which he served last, and this Church shall provide honourably for his support. The same obligation exists towards a minister's widow and/or dependants. Retirement of a minister shall take place with the approval of the consistory with the deacons and with the concurring advice of classis and the deputies of regional synod.

Dealing with several appeals and letters regarding the revision of the Church Order, the General Synod Burlington-West 1986 adopted this version of Article 13, which more or less means a return to what had been in use until the General Synod Cloverdale 1983.

As Article 12 put it, a minister is bound to the service of the church for life. However, there can be certain reasons why he will no longer be able to discharge the duties of his office to the fullest extent.

The first reason is that of age. In some of our foreign sister churches ministers have the right to retire at the age of sixty-five.

Another reason is illness, or physical or mental disability.

The nature of the retirement of a minister of the Word is such that he is relieved from the duties of his office.

However, a retired minister remains a minister, and can occasionally be invited to preach God's Word, administer the sacraments, etc.

Another consequence of the principle that he is and remains a minister, is that the church he has served until his retirement must continue his financial support.

40

It is a matter of course that the same obligations also applies to widows and dependants of ministers.

Usually the honorarium of a retired minister is less than that of an active minister. In this connection it is sometimes forgotten that at their retirement most ministers are not in a position to buy a house for themselves. It would be a good thing if the consistories would make timely provisions in this respect.

Another consequence of the above-mentioned principle is that the minister-emeritus, in comparison to the minister who is called to replace him, is the "first" and the latter the "second" minister.

This means that if a congregation were to run into difficulties in financially supporting both ministers, she would have to request the assistance of the sister churches for the financial support of the replacing minister.

Retirement procedure is as follows:

1. The minister requests his consistory in writing to relieve him of the duties of his office, giving the reasons for this request.
2. The consistory, having considered these reasons, grants him this request and declares him minister-emeritus at a time agreed upon by both parties; and issues to him a certificate regarding this.
3. Classis is informed and requested to approve the action, with the support of the deputies of the regional synod appointed for this purpose.
4. Classis and the deputies see to it that there are sufficient reasons to declare the minister concerned emeritus, and they make sure that the consistory will indeed support the minister-emeritus honourably.
5. A certificate is issued by the classis and the deputies to both the minister and the consistory.

ARTICLE 14. Temporary Release

> *If a minister, because of illness or for other substantial reasons, requests a temporary release from his service to the congregation, he can receive the same only with the approval of the consistory with the deacons and shall at all times be and remain subject to the call of the congregation.*

The illness mentioned in the previous article can be of a temporary character. In the meantime it can be so serious as to make it impossible for the minister to discharge the duties of his office for some time.

This and other substantial reasons — such as a special study which could be beneficial to the church — may cause him to request a temporary release from his service.

Since this is a temporary release only, the approval of the consistory — again with the deacons — is sufficient. It is not necessary to involve the classis and the deputies of the regional synod.

Special circumstances may lead the consistory to terminate this release — as a matter of course, the minister's health permitting.

ARTICLE 15. Preaching in Other Places

> *No one shall be permitted to preach the Word or to administer the Sacraments in another Church without the consent of the consistory of that Church.*

Our ministers are not ministers of a "national church" or of the federation of churches, but of the local congregation only.

This is the underlying principle of Article 15, a principle that was also expressed in Article 6.

Consequently a minister can preach the Word of God and administer the sacraments in another congregation only with the permission of the consistory of that church.

Of course, this permission is included in an invitation to serve as a guest-preacher.

ARTICLE 16. The Office of the Ministers of the Word

> *The specific duties of the office of minister of the Word are thoroughly and sincerely to proclaim to the congregation the Word of the Lord; to administer the sacraments; publicly to call upon the Name of God in behalf of the whole congregation; also to instruct the children of the Church in the doctrine of salvation, to visit the members of the congregation in their homes, and to comfort the sick with the Word of God; and further, with the elders, to keep the Church of God in good order, to exercise discipline, and to govern it in such a manner as the Lord has ordained.*

This article and also Articles 22 and 23 have in their title the word "office." This means that a higher authority has appointed the bearers of these offices: they are called by Christ, the Head of the church, through His congregation.

The contents of this article are an elaboration on what we confess in our Belgic Confession of Faith, Article 10: "There should be ministers or pastors to preach the Word of God and to administer the sacraments."

Its formulation is closely related to Lord's Day 38 of the Heidelberg Catechism.

As for the minister's first-mentioned task, it would be wise to take to heart the warning issued by Van Dellen and Monsma, in their *Revised Church Order Commentary*, 1969, p. 57:

> And this beautiful and meaningful task of explaining and applying God's holy Word may indeed be classified as the minister's primary task and responsibility. Well may every one called to this task heed with holy fear the apostle's word to Timothy: "Preach the Word!" (II Timothy 4:2). This point cannot be

42

stressed too strongly in our day. Addresses on secular subjects may not take the place of sermons based on God's own Word. Neither should we be satisfied if the minister should deliver excellent religious addresses. Topical sermons are very often little more than religious discourses, in which the preacher's opinion looms up large. What we should demand without wavering, is exposition and application of God's own Word. Religious discourses are often much more popular with the crowd than regular sermons. But in the interest of the spiritual welfare of our members and the future of our churches we should continue to insist on expository sermons. Of course this does not mean that our sermons should not be practical. A good sermon *expounds* and *applies* God's special revelation.

Since the proclaiming of God's Word has been entrusted to the ministers, it will be clear that the administration of the sacraments — ''the visible Word'' (John Calvin) — is another aspect of their task.

The third element mentioned in this article is that of leading in the public prayers. During the church services — which have an antiphonal, covenantal character — the minister does not only represent God to the congregation, but he also addresses the LORD on behalf of the congregation. This requires a good preparation — just as the whole of the church service requires this: a minister should not only prepare his sermon, but the service as a whole!

A minister is not only a preacher but also a teacher. One of his tasks is to instruct the children of the congregation.

We may again quote Van Dellen and Monsma (op.cit, p.58), when they say:

In many denominations all around us on the American continent we see the tragic result of the gross failure of churches to indoctrinate their children and young people properly. Humanly speaking it may be said that if these churches had maintained a strong and effective catechetical program, modernism and the sects never would have succeeded in ruining the churches to the tragic extent to which they have been ruined. A thorough knowledge of the doctrinal truths revealed to us in the Bible is as essential to the well-being and continuance of any church, as the framework of any dwelling is to the well-being and continuance of the building.

For very good reasons God has seen fit to deposit the doctrinal truths regarding the way of salvation for us in His Word. He can only ignore and neglect these truths at the expense of the church's well-being and of its very life as a true Church of Christ. The thorough indoctrination of the youth of the churches constitutes a large part of our main line of defense against liberalism, sectarianism, and all kinds of inferior, false, and soul-destroying conceptions.

As for the fourth element mentioned in this article, it does not only refer to the visits by the minister on his own, let alone to visits in some "special cases," but it also allows for his taking part in the home visits made by the elders — which has proven to be very useful to the other element in his ministry.

As for the last part of the minister's task, this article again refers to the Scriptural foundation of the Church Order, I Corinthians 14:40: "All things should be done decently and in order."

A further exposition of the duties of the minister's office is given in the Form for the Ordination (or Installation) of Ministers of the Word.

ARTICLE 17. Equality among the Ministers of the Word

Among the ministers of the Word equality shall be maintained with respect to the duties of their office and in other matters as far as possible, according to the judgment of the consistory, and, if necessary, of classis.

This article again is of a confessional character. Our Belgic Confession says in Article 31:

> Ministers of the Word, in whatever place they are, have equal power and authority, for they are all servants of Jesus Christ, the only universal Bishop and the only Head of the Church.

This is confessed in opposition to the hierarchy in the "episcopal churches," such as the church of Rome, the church of England, and the Lutheran churches.

It is based on Matthew 18:1-4 and parallel texts, on the answer of the Saviour given to the disciples' question: "Who is the greatest in the kingdom of heaven?":

> Truly, I say to you, unless you turn and become like children, you will never enter the kingdom of heaven. Whoever humbles himself like this child, he is the greatest in the kingdom of heaven.

This is why the Reformed churches have no bishops, superintendents, et al.

There must be equality:

1. in the execution of the office. When there are two or more ministers, the one should not be given the task of preaching, the other that of visiting the church members, and so on. Even the position of chairman of the consistory shall be shared, e.g. on a monthly basis.
2. in all other respects, e.g. regarding the honorarium — although

special circumstances have to be taken into consideration, e.g. the number of a minister's children.

The consistory shall see to it that the workload is equally divided among its ministers.

If this would create any problems, the classis can provide help — although we have never heard that this was needed.

It is finally added that the same rule applies to elders and deacons.

All this is, in a sense, repeated in Article 80.

ARTICLE 18. Missionaries

> *When ministers of the Word are sent out as missionaries, they shall be and remain subject to the Church Order. They shall report and give account of their labours to the Church which sent them and shall at all times remain subject to its calling.*
>
> *It shall be their task, in the specific region assigned to them or chosen by them in consultation with the Church that sent them, to proclaim the Word of God, to administer the sacraments to those who have come to the profession of their faith, teaching them to observe all that Christ has commanded His Church, and to ordain elders and deacons when this appears feasible, according to the rules given in the Word of God.*

Two principles are at the background of this article. The first one is that mission work is not the task of individuals or of mission societies and suchlike; this calling is a calling of the churches.

Missionaries were mentioned in Article 6 already. It was stated there that they are bound to a church. Therefore Article 18 says that they are subject to the Church Order. This means, e.g., that they must be lawfully called (Article 3); that, having been ordained or installed according to Article 5, they cannot leave their service without the permission and approval of the consistory and classis (Article 9), and that they are bound to the service of the church for life (Article 12).

Another consequence of being bound to a certain church is that they shall report and give account of their labours to the ''sending Church.''

The second underlying principle is that the aim of mission work is not only to call individuals to conversion and faith, but also to plant the church of the Lord Jesus Christ.

Therefore the task of the missionaries is, in accordance with Matthew 28:18-20:

1. to proclaim God's Word in their ''mission field.''
2. to administer the sacraments to those who have come to faith as a result of the mission work.
3. to teach them to observe all that Christ commanded His church — which includes a Christian life-style.

4. to institute the offices according to good order.

Mission work has been undertaken by the following "sending Churches" — which are assisted by churches in their region — : Toronto in Irian Jaya, Hamilton and Surrey in Brazil.

ARTICLE 19. Training for the Ministry

The Churches shall maintain an institution for the training for the ministry. The task of the professors of theology is to instruct the students of theology in those disciplines which have been entrusted to them, so that the Churches may be provided with ministers of the Word who are able to fulfill the duties of their office as these have been described before.

A few times we have already made mention of the Theological College at Hamilton. This institute was established in the year 1969 and has since then been maintained in accordance with this article. It has proven to be a great blessing for our churches, for it has provided the churches with capable ministers.

The composition of the teaching staff fully complies with the text of this article, which speaks of "professors of theology." This, however, does not exclude the possibility that part-time lecturers render their assistance, as indeed was done in the past.

This article uses even twice the word "theology," in "professors of theology" and "students of theology." Theology is a science that as its field of inquiry has God's revelation, as it:

1. is contained in Holy Scriptures:
   the bibliological section, with the following subjects:
   The text of the Old and New Testament;
   Canonics;
   History of the revelation;
   Biblical history;
   Hermeneutics;
   Exegesis;
2. gives shape to the church:
   the ecclesiological section, with these subjects:
   Church history;
   Church polity;
3. is confessed in the dogma:
   the dogmatological section:
   Symbolics (creeds and confessions);
   Systematic theology;
   Ethics;
4. is proclaimed by the ecclesiastical office:
   the diaconological section:
   Homiletics;
   Catechetics;
   Liturgics;
   Poimenics;
   Diaconics.

Missiology and Evangelistics are included in this section.

At the Theological College, Hamilton, these disciplines are taught by the following professors respectively: Dr. C. Van Dam (Old Testament), J. Geertsema (New Testament), Dr. J. Faber (section 3), and Dr. K. Deddens (sections 2 and 4).

Recently a "special missionary training" has been established in addition to the regular program.

Article 19 suggest that the training for the ministry of the Word ends as soon as one has passed the final examination at the College. However, such an institution should open the possibility for ministers to continue their theological studies until the degree of "doctor of theology" is obtained.

The supervision over the college is in the hands of a Board of Governors appointed by general synod.

Although the Church Order does not expressly state it, the professors of theology are ministers who have been set apart for the training of students.

They therefore remain bound to the church which they last served, and keep their position as ministers.

ARTICLE 20. Students of Theology

The Churches shall endeavour that there be students of theology, extending financial aid to those who are in need of it.

This article, then, does not exclusively deal with the financial aid extended to students of theology, who are not in a position to finance such a study, or have it financed e.g. by their parents.

First of all it contains a clause regarding the task of the churches. It shows that the availability of a continuous supply of able young men desiring to train for the ministry should have the constant attention of the churches.

The expense involved usually makes it impossible for one single congregation to extend financial support when the parents are not in a position to provide it. The formulation of this article, then, suggests that the necessary aid is extended by the churches in general, either through classis or regional synod, for which purpose deputies are appointed.

It does not suggest that the financial aid must be refunded later on.

ARTICLE 21. An Edifying Word

Besides those who have been permitted, according to Article 8, to speak an edifying word, also others may be given such consent in accordance with general ecclesiastical regulations, for their own training and in order that they may become known in the congregations.

The General Synod New Westminster 1971 had to deal with a number of requests from within the churches to grant students of theology the right to speak an edifying word in the churches under certain conditions.

Synod decided (Acts, Article 76):

> that students of theology may receive the right to speak an edifying word in the Churches on the following conditions:
> 1. They shall submit the request for such permission to the Classis.
> 2. They shall not do so unless they have completed at least two years of theological studies.
> 3. They shall present a good attestation from the Church to which they belong.
> 4. They shall present a certificate from the Faculty of our Theological College that they have satisfactorily completed at least two years of studies at the College.
> 5. They shall deliver a sermon at the Classis and shall be interrogated on the Reformed doctrine.
> 6. If, as a result of this examination, the Classis decides to grant their request, permission shall be given for a period not exceeding twelve months, and that under the condition that the student shall submit his sermons to and discuss them with the Lecturer in the Diaconological department at our College.

Since the General Synod Toronto 1974 decided to instruct the Board of Governors to extend the Course of Studies from three to four years, to be effective as of the beginning of the Academic Year 1975-1976 (Acts, Article 171 sub B6), only students who have completed three years of studies at the College are allowed to speak an edifying word in the churches.

General Synod Cloverdale 1983 decided to include an article regarding this issue in the Church Order.

ARTICLE 22. The Office of Elder

The specific duties of the office of elder are: together with the ministers of the Word, to have supervision over Christ's Church, that every member may conduct himself properly in doctrine and life according to the gospel; faithfully to visit the members of the congregation in their homes to comfort, instruct, and admonish them with the Word of God, reproving those who behave improperly. They shall exercise Christian discipline according to the command of Christ against those who show themselves unbelieving and ungodly and refuse to repent; they shall watch that the sacraments are not profaned. They further are to take care, being stewards of the house of God, that in the congregation all things are done decently and in good order, and to tend the flock of Christ which is in their charge. Final-

ly, it is their duty to assist the ministers of the Word with good counsel and advice and to supervise their doctrine and conduct.

First a general description of the task of elders is given: Together with the ministers they shall be the pastors of the congregation. This includes:

1. making homevisits. It does not say how often these visits must be made, but the word "faithfully" makes it perfectly clear that they must not be limited to one each year to every "address," but should be more frequent whenever necessary.

   These homevisits shall consist of comfort, instruction, and admonition.

   All this must be done "with the Word of God." Therefore it is advisable to begin with Scripture-reading, which should be followed by a few sentences — not a "sermon"! — intended to open a good discussion.

   It is also advisable that the children of school-going age and older be present, although the home-visits are not intended as an examination of their Bible-knowledge and suchlike.

   The visiting elders shall see to it that every member of the family present is included in the discussion.

   Older children who have already made their public profession of faith may be visited separately.

   It would be wise to divide the congregation into as many sections or wards as there are elders, so that each elder will be able to keep a special eye on those who have been particularly entrusted to his care.

   In the meantime it should be clear that each elder is an elder of the whole congregation.

2. exercising church discipline, together with the ministers. This includes taking watch that the sacraments are not profaned.

3. seeing to it that everything in the congregation is done "decently and in good order" — which is another reference to the apostolic command of I Corinthians 14:40, the foundation of our Church Order.

4. assisting the ministers with good counsel and advice, and supervising their doctrine and conduct.

   A discussion, of the minister's preaching every now and then arranged at a consistory meeting, may be useful if it is limited to the question whether his sermons are in harmony with the doctrine of the church, as well as restricted to this "good advice."

ARTICLE 23. The Office of Deacon

The specific duties of the office of deacon are: to see to the good progress of the service of charity in the congregation; to acquaint themselves with existing needs and difficulties, and to exhort the members of Christ's body to show mercy; further, to gather and manage the offerings and to distribute them in Christ's Name according to need. They shall encourage and comfort with the Word of God those who receive the gifts of Christ's love, and promote with word and deed the unity and fellowship in the Holy Spirit which the congregation enjoys at the table of the Lord.

The final clause of this article reminds us of the origin of the office of deacon, and of the close relationship between his task and the unity of the congregation as expressed at the Table of the Lord.

The "serving tables" of Acts 6:2 is a matter of care for the indigent, and not of assisting in the celebration of the Mass, as e.g. in the church of Rome.

Our Church Order calls it "the service of charity."

This ministry shall not only be performed to the "poor." This article speaks of "difficulties," of which there can be various kinds: e.g., older or lonely people may need special help.

Therefore the deacons must visit, help, and encourage where there is need, but also urge church members to render assistance. They do not have to do these things all by themselves — or with the help of their wives! They have to see to it that the congregation is in this respect indeed a "communion of saints" according to Heidelberg Catechism, Lord's Day 21.

Because part of their duties has a financial aspect, they have to collect the gifts, take charge of them, and distribute them where there is need. The latter shall be done after mutual consultation, for which purpose they shall regularly come together (Article 40).

The collecting of gifts normally takes place during the church services. However, in urgent cases the deacons may have to visit the members of the congregation, or some who are well-off, and ask them for extra gifts.

We cannot deal here with the liturgical aspect of the collections, but would like to make one single remark concerning them: The number of circulating collection-bags is to be increased as soon as the offerings are going to take more than two or three minutes.

From the description of the task of the deacons it may be clear that this office has its own significance and difficulties.

We therefore should not consider it a promotion when someone who before used to be a deacon is appointed and ordained as an elder.

After having served for the appointed time (Article 23), a retired deacon shall be given the same period of rest as other retired office-bearers, and not be immediately nominated for the office of elder.

For the same reason the deacons shall not be requisitioned from among the younger members only — compared with the average age of the elders.

Our Church Order does not count the deacons among the members of the consistory, except in the case mentioned in Article 39.

The question whether this is in harmony with Article 30 of the Belgic Confession of Faith cannot be dealt with here. It seems as if the Confession considers the deacons as full members of the consistory.

However, this does not mean that according to our Confession the deacons are expected to attend all the meetings of the ministers and elders that are arranged to discuss their respective tasks as they are explained in Article 30. Our Church Order makes mention of certain consistory meetings whereby the deacons are supposed to be present (Articles 3, 5B, 9, 10, 11, 12, 13, 14, 24, 26, 71).

In practical church life this discrepancy between the formulation of our Church Order and that of our Confession is not a real problem.

See further our comment on Article 39.

ARTICLE 24. Term of Office

The elders and deacons shall serve two or more years according to local regulations, and a proportionate number shall retire each year. The place of the retiring office-bearers shall be taken by others, unless the consistory with the deacons judges that the circumstances and the benefit of the Church render it advisable to have them serve another term, or to extend their term, or to declare them immediately eligible for re-election.

Holy Scripture gives us no indication regarding the duration of the term elders and deacons should serve in their respective offices.

Our Reformed churches have deemed it wise not to introduce the "life-long" or "permanent" elder or deacon. The main reason for this is the wish to prevent a certain form of hierarchy from creeping into congregational life.

Our churches, however, have agreed to determine the minimum term of office at two years. The congregations keep their freedom not to restrict themselves to this minimum.

Another rule agreed to is that each year a proportional number of elders and deacons shall retire.

Article 3 already dealt with the calling of elders and deacons who can replace them. However, in certain instances it could be desirable and useful for the well-being of the congregation if all or some retiring office-bearers were able to continue their work in the midst of the congregation. In this case three different options are summed up: they could serve another full term; their term of office could be extended (say, by one year); or the consistory could declare them immediately eligible for re-election. In the last mentioned case the normal procedure explained in Article 3 is followed.

ARTICLE 25. Equality to be Maintained

Among the elders as well as among the deacons equality shall be maintained with respect to the duties of their office, and also, as far as possible, in other matters, of which the consistory shall judge.

This article is similar to that regarding the ministers (Art. 17).

Although some of the elders and deacons have more time available than others, this should not lead to the creation of "frontbenchers" and "backbenchers."

Unlike in Article 17, no mention is made of classis involvement "if necessary," which is due to the fact that ministers are "fulltime" and take a special position within the federation of churches.

ARTICLE 26. Subscription to the Confession

All ministers of the Word, elders, deacons, and professors of theology shall subscribe to the Confessions of the Canadian Reformed Churches by signing the form(s) adopted for that purpose.

Anyone refusing to subscribe in that manner shall not be ordained or installed in office. Anyone who, being in office, refuses to do so shall, because of that very fact, be immediately suspended from office by the consistory with the deacons, and classis shall not receive him; and if he obstinately persists in his refusal, he shall be deposed from office.

The first point in the supervision over doctrine is the subscription to the Three Forms of Unity by the ministers, the professors and other lecturers at the Theological College; i.e., by all those who, directly or indirectly, are involved in the preaching of God's Word.

The churches have to be absolutely sure that all fully agree with the Scriptural doctrine confessed in the Three Forms of Unity.

Even the candidates to the Ministry, immediately after having passed their peremptory examination, have to subscribe to them (Article 5).

The subscription to the Belgic Confession of Faith by ministers, elders, and deacons, dates back to the year 1563, two years after it was published by Guido de Brès. This practice was adopted by a provincial synod held at Armentières in French Flanders. Other provincial synods in the Southern Netherlands followed suit.

In the year 1568 the Convent of Wesel took a similar decision, also including the Heidelberg Catechism. The first synod of the Dutch churches, held in 1571 at Emden, issued the following statement: "In order to prove the concord among the Dutch Churches concerning the confession, the brethren decided it to be proper to subscribe to the Confession of Faith of the Dutch Churches."

The Canons of Dort were included in this subscription at the National Synod of Dordrecht 1618-1619.

Since then, the subscription form for ministers contains the following elements:
1. a clear declaration that the doctrine of the Three Forms of Unity is in every respect in conformity with the Word of God;
2. the solemn promise to teach this doctrine and faithfully to promote it, and to reject, refute, and resist all errors in contradiction with it, without teaching or writing openly or secretly, directly or indirectly, anything against it;
3. the clear promise that if one would conceive any thought or feeling against the aforesaid doctrine or any point of it, this will never be openly or secretly presented, promoted or written, but that it will first be submitted to the classis or synod for examination;
4. the promise, if consistory, classis or synod would for important reasons deem it proper to demand more explicit explanations, to be willing to give them, on penalty of immediate suspension from service.

There are a number of different forms, drawn up for the various offices. However, fundamentally they are all the same.

If a minister refuses to sign, the consistory shall immediately suspend him, and the classis — entry to which is obtained by subscription to the doctrine of the churches — shall not receive him.

The minister concerned then receives the opportunity to explain his deviating opinions. If he, however, persists in his refusal to subscribe as yet, he shall be deposed from his office.

The subscription form for ministers even includes a clause stating that if a consistory, classis, or synod, for good reasons requires a further exposition of one's views, for the preservation of the unity and purity of doctrine the minister must be willing to give it. These "good reasons" are, of course, to be based on certain utterances of the minister concerned.

This is another regulation and practice intended to keep the churches in conformity with the Word of God, so that they may remain true and faithful churches of the Lord Jesus Christ. For the first mark of the true church is, according to Article 29 of the Belgic Confession of Faith: "It practises the pure preaching of the gospel."

All that has been said in Article 50 in respect to ministers, and professors, at the Theological College, can be applied to the elders and deacons. They, too, at the beginning of their term of office, have to subscribe to the Three Forms of Unity.

Many church groups, after originally having adopted a Scriptural confession, have, in the course of time, weakened their stand by requiring subscription to a form which leaves the door open to all sorts of views that deviate from the official creeds and confessions. This is sometimes defended with the help of all sorts of theories concerning the value of a confession. One of the most recent theories is that the confession expresses the religious feelings of the church at the time when it was written, but that these feelings are subject to evolution, so that in our modern times no one can be bound to the literal text of the official doctrinal standards.

Up till today the LORD, in His mercy, has kept us free from ideas of this kind!

ARTICLE 27. False Doctrine

To ward off false doctrines and errors which could enter the congregation and constitute a danger to the purity of its doctrine or conduct, the ministers and elders shall use the means of instruction, of refutation, of warning, and of admonition, as well in the ministry of the Word as in Christian teaching and family visiting.

In the early days the Church Order contained an article on a sort of censorship: No religious publications were allowed without the permission of the ministers in the classis, the province, or the professors of theology, the classis being informed.

The Reformed churches, however — unlike the church of Rome — could not maintain this stand.

Meanwhile, it is of great significance that the churches are protected against false doctrine and errors. Therefore it is expressly emphasized by means of this article that there is here a special task for the ministers and elders.

Consequently they must keep themselves well informed. Which means that a minister's honorarium must allow him to purchase the necessary books and subscribe to various periodicals.

The churches themselves would be well advised to establish a "church library," so as to enable all office-bearers and other members to remain up to date in the affairs of the churches.

They must all be able, in the preaching of the Word, at catechism classes, and during the home visits, to teach and warn the members of the congregation against heresies and errors.

ARTICLE 28. Civil Authorities

As it is the office of the civil authorities to promote in every way the holy ministry, so all office-bearers are in duty bound to impress diligently and sincerely upon the whole congregation the obedience, love, and respect which are due to the civil authorities; they shall set a good example to the whole congregation in this matter, and endeavour by due respect and communication to secure and retain the favour of the authorities towards the Church, so that the Church of Christ may lead a quiet and peaceable life, godly and respectful in every way.

This is another article in the Church Order that is clearly of a confessional character. It emphasizes the consequences for our church life of the confession contained in Article 36 of the Belgic

54

Confession of Faith, that "because of the depravity of mankind, our gracious God has ordained kings, princes and civil officers."

Besides, Article 27 starts with referring to our Confession, which says concerning civil authorities:

> Their task of restraining and sustaining is not limited to the public order but includes the protection of the Church and its ministry.

This is the basis on which rest the clauses which follow. There are two sections:

1. on the attitude of the congregation towards the civil government, and the duty of the office-bearers in this respect.
2. on the duties of the office-bearers themselves concerning the civil government.

Re 1:

The office-bearers must see to it that a Christian attitude towards civil authorities is shown by the congregation: obedience, love and respect are due to them — which is in accordance with the teachings of the Bible, e.g. in Romans 13:1.

The consistory as a body is not mentioned in this article; it speaks of "all office-bearers." This may emphasize that each office-bearer has an individual task here.

Re 2:

The duties of the office-bearers themselves are twofold:

a. They themselves have to be good examples of obedience and of love and respect for the government.
b. They may have to contact the government — communicating with them in a respectful way — in order that, in accordance with I Timothy 2:2, the church of Christ may lead a quiet and peaceable life, godly and respectful in every way.

III. The Assemblies

> *Four kinds of ecclesiastical assemblies shall be maintained: The Consistory, the Classis, the Regional Synod, and the General Synod.*

It is not strange that the part of the Church Order which deals with the assemblies immediately follows the section on the offices.

For our Church Order is not first of all intended to serve as a set of rules for local use but as the formulation of what the churches in general have agreed upon.

Again we must say that our Church Order has a confessional character, and is a kind of elaboration on a specific theme in our Three Forms of Unity. Actually there are two themes involved; both are very closely related. The first is found in our Heidelberg Catechism, Q.&A. 54:

> What do you believe concerning the holy catholic church of Christ?
>
> I believe that the Son of God, out of the whole human race, from the beginning of the world to its end, gathers, defends, and preserves for Himself, by His Spirit and Word, in the unity of true faith, a church chosen to everlasting life.

It is also found in our Belgic Confession of Faith, Article 27, which reads:

> We believe and profess one catholic or universal Church, which is a holy congregation and assembly of the true Christian believers, who expect their entire salvation in Jesus Christ, are washed by His blood, and are sanctified and sealed by the Holy Spirit. . . . Moreover, this holy Church is not confined or limited to one particular place or to certain persons, but is spread and dispersed throughout the entire world. However, it is joined and united with heart and will, in one and the same Spirit by the power of faith.

The last-quoted sentence shows us again that our Church Order is of a confessional character. Article 30 of the Belgic Confession expresses its obedience to the apostolic command of I Corinthians 14:40: "All things should be done decently and in order." The Church Order, having this command as its theme, is a further elaboration on the confession.

This, then, is the same church concerning which we confess (Article 28) that

> all and everyone are obliged to join it and unite with it, maintaining the unity of the Church. They must submit themselves to its instruction and discipline.

This church is known by its marks (Article 29):

It practices the pure preaching of the gospel. It maintains the pure administration of the sacraments as Christ instituted them. It exercises Church discipline for correcting and punishing sins. In short, it governs itself according to the pure Word of God, rejecting all things contrary to it and regarding Jesus Christ as the only Head. Hereby the true Church can certainly be known and no one has the right to separate from it.

It

must be governed according to the Spiritual order which our Lord has taught us in His Word. There should be ministers or pastors to preach the Word of God and to administer the sacraments; there should also be elders and deacons who, together with the pastors, for the council of the Church. By these means they preserve the true religion; they see to it that the true doctrine takes its course, that evil men are disciplined in a spiritual way and are restrained, and also that the poor and all the afflicted are helped and comforted according to their need. By these means everything will be done well and in good order when faithful men are chosen in agreement with the rule that the apostle Paul gave to Timothy. (Article 30.)

The consequence of all this for practical church life is that we must take our starting-point in the local church — although not in the sense of the Independentists.

Besides, the consistory is the only ecclesiastical assembly that is mentioned in Scripture and was ordained by Christ's apostles. I Timothy 4:14 speaks of ''the council of elders'' — which is a translation (RSV) of the original Greek word *presbyterion*. Other places in Scripture also refer to the elders as a body: Acts 20:17, 28; I Timothy 5:17; I Peter 5:1-3; cf. Matthew 16:19.

This, then, is the first theme of our confessional writings on which our Church Order elaborates.

The second is that of the unity of faith, and consequently the unity of the church.

This is again based on Holy Scripture, which emphasizes the unity of the Spirit (Ephesians 4:3) in the one body, under the one Lord, with the one baptism (4:4,5). Our Saviour prayed that those who would learn to believe in Him through the word of the apostles would be one (John 17: 20f.)

The church is a whole body. She is Christ's body (Colossians 1:18; cf. Belgic Confession of Faith, Article 28; and Heidelberg Catechism, Lord's Day 21, Q.&A. 54).

Holy Scripture, then, does indicate that the separate congregations must keep themselves informed about the situation in their sister churches and learn from their circumstances. Christ's royal words to each of the seven congregations in Asia Minor had to be read, together with the whole book of Revelation, in the other six churches as well (Revelation 2:7, 11, 17, 29; 3:6, 13, 22). The Apostle Paul's epistle to the Colossians also had to be read in the congregation at Laodicea, and the other way round (Colossians 4:16).

On the basis of all this, the Church Order distinguishes between four ecclesiastical assemblies:

1. the consistory.
2. the classis.
3. the regional synod.
4. the general synod.

Re 1:

The consistory consists of ministers and elders. It is the only assembly directly based on Holy Scripture.

Articles 38-41 will further deal with the consistory.

Re 2:

The classis consists of delegates from the consistories of churches in a certain region.

Like the regional and general synods, we call it a major assembly, which does not mean that it is a higher authority with more power, but simply an assembly formed by a larger number of churches through their representatives.

The name "classis," has been derived from a Greek and a Latin word which means "to call together."

The articles of Wesel, 1568, advised the creation of classes

for the establishing and preserving of consensus in doctrine, ceremonies, and church discipline, and for common actions and mutual consultation in matters of importance regarding common interests.

Articles 44-46 will further deal with the classis.

At the moment there are four classes: Classis Ontario-North, Classis Ontario-South, Classis Alberta-Manitoba, and Classis Pacific.

Re 3:

The regional synod is an assembly consisting of delegates sent by each classis.

For further particulars we may refer to Articles 47 and 48.

At the moment there are two regional synods: Regional Synod East, to which the classes Ontario-North and Ontario-South send their delegates, and Regional Synod West, to which the other two classes send their representatives.

Re 4:

The general synod is an assembly consisting of delegates sent by the regional synods.

Every now and then an effort is made to base this assembly,

or its equivalent in other churches, on Acts 15:6. However, this "Jerusalem meeting" was of a different nature. It consisted of the apostles and the elders of the congregation of Jerusalem. The young churches were in need of some advice and even rules, given them by Christ's apostles and the leaders of the "mother church." This meeting was different from those held later on when church life had become well organized, in accordance with e.g. the Pastoral Epistles of the Apostle Paul. The "Jerusalem meeting" was definitely not a synod!

Our Church Order does not make mention of an "international" or "ecumenical" synod or council.

However, some efforts were made during the sixteenth century to call such a meeting together.

John Calvin was strongly in favour of it, as may be proven from his correspondence with Thomas Cranmer and Johann Heinrich Bullinger. He even wrote:

> I would not shrink from crossing ten seas, should that be necessary, for the purpose of attending such a gathering. . . . I am of the opinion that neither energy nor pains should be spared.

Some action of this effect was undertaken by Queen Elizabeth I of England. She wanted all the Protestants to establish a league, whereby she herself, the Huguenots, and the Dutch Protestants would be protected against the church of Rome. Her efforts failed, however, but one of the envoys she had sent to the European continent visited Count John Casimir of the Palatinate, a meeting which led to the convening of the Convention of Frankfurt, 1577. This convention made some arrangements for the composition of a common confession for all the Reformed churches, those of France, of the Netherlands, Switzerland, Poland, England, and Scotland. Its draft was, however, not acceptable to the church at Geneva, but a *Harmonia Confessionum*, a collection of all the Reformed confessions, was published in the year 1581.

In Scotland and England the desire to have international meetings was recorded in a number of official documents.

"The Second Book of Discipline" of the church of Scotland, 1578, mentions four ecclesiastical assemblies: one consisting of "particular kirkis and congregationis," another of a province, a third one of the whole nation, and finally "of all and divers nationis professing ane Jesus Chryst."

The English "Book of Discipline," 1578, finishes with the following sentence:

> Thus much for particular meetings, the universal followeth, which is called a general or oecumenical council, which is a meeting of the chosen men of every national synod.

"The Form of Presbyterial Church-Government," the Presbyterian Church Order, which dates back to the year 1645, states under the heading "Of Synodical Assemblies":

Synodical assemblies may lawfully be of several sorts, as provincial, national, and oecumenical.

At the same time of the National Synod of Dordrecht 1618/19 a new plan was made.

The plan included an international assembly that would write one single Reformed confession for all the churches. The name of Pierre du Moulin, a Frenchman, is connected with it, as also that of King James I of England.

The Synod of Dordrecht, however, did not officially discuss it, but it was discussed in the lobbies.

Du Moulin, who had been delegated to "Dort" by the French churches, and with his fellow-delegates were forbidden by the king of France to leave for the Netherlands.

We do not intend to make a plea for the adding of an "ecumenical synod" as a fourth ecclesiastical assembly to our Church Order. An international conference may be sufficient in maintaining contact between sister churches and dealing with common affairs.

In the year 1982 a Constituent Assembly for an International Conference of Reformed Churches (I.C.R.C.) was held at Groningen, the Netherlands. The first Conference was held in 1985 at Edinburgh, Scotland. It appointed two study committees, one with the mandate "to study the text of the three ecumenical Creeds in order to come to a common text that can be recommended to the member Churches," another with the mandate "(i) to gather information from the member Churches regarding their missionary activities and training programs; (ii) to study the possibilities of coordinating the missionary activities of the member Churches when it comes to training, mission fields and exchanging missionaries; (iii) to examine the need to produce listings of relevant missionary literature on an ongoing basis, and to promote the publication of an introduction to Reformed missions."

The second Conference is to be convened by the Canadian Reformed Churches and held, the LORD willing, in the summer/autumn of 1989 in the Vancouver area.

At their General Synod Cloverdale 1983 the Canadian Reformed Churches decided to join the I.C.R.C.

ARTICLE 30. Ecclesiastical Matters

These assemblies shall deal with no other than ecclesiastical matters and that in an ecclesiastical manner.

A major assembly shall deal with those matters only which could not be finished in the minor assembly or which belong to its Churches in common.

A new matter which has not previously been presented to that major assembly may be put on the agenda only when the minor assembly has dealt with it.

This article deals with the agenda of, respectively:
1. all the assemblies.
2. the major assemblies.

Re 1:

Before and during the first stages of the Eighty Years War (1568-1648) the Dutch churches occasionally kept themselves occupied with all sorts of non-ecclesiastical matters; e.g. with questions like these: Are we allowed to defend ourselves against the persecuting papists by force or arms? Are we allowed to free those who have been imprisoned for the sake of their faith? Can we as churches support the uprising against Spain, for example by collecting funds for hiring mercenaries or by passing on military secrets?

But since the National Synod of Middelburg, 1581, the present rule has been adopted and maintained.

The churches should not occupy themselves with all sorts of matters either of an economic, social, political, or scientific nature. They shall restrict themselves to ecclesiastical matters like doctrinal affairs, church discipline, the maintaining of good order in the churches, etc.

This shall be done "in an ecclesiastical manner," which means: not by command, or by force, but by convincing, admonishing, and ruling according to God's Word.

Re 2:

The agenda of the major assemblies is determined by two groups of subjects:
a. those matters which could not be resolved in the minor assemblies; e.g. appeals.
b. matters which concern the churches in common; e.g. the training for the ministry of the Word.

The matters mentioned under a. are casual. Those mentioned under b. shall be put on the agenda of the major assembly by the convening church.

The revision of the Church Order at the General Synod Cloverdale 1983 added a sentence to clarify the way in which a certain matter can be placed on the agenda of a major assembly: only by preparation in the minor assemblies.

This means in the first place that the delegates of a consistory or of a classis and regional synod cannot put anything on the agenda of either classis or regional synod and general synod respectively, at their own initiative.

Even a local church cannot have a certain matter put on the agenda of a classis unless the other classical churches have had the opportunity to study it.

If a local church would like a certain matter put on the agenda of general synod, it must first of all be dealt with "in the ecclesiastical way," by the classis and the regional synod. Via the draft agenda which the convening church of the general synod sends to all the churches they do have the opportunity to study the material. According to Article 31 appeals are excepted from this rule.

ARTICLE 31. Appeals

> *If anyone complains that he has been wronged by the decision of a minor assembly, he shall have the right to appeal to the major ecclesiastical assembly; and whatever may be agreed upon by a majority vote shall be considered settled and binding, unless it is proved to be in conflict with the Word of God or with the Church Order.*

This is an essential article in our Church Order. It is intended to serve the peace and order in the churches. We can say: It is founded on the Apostle Paul's words in I Corinthians 14:33: "God is not a God of confusion but of peace," which is the basis also of that other text in which our Church Order has its very roots (14:40): "All things should be done decently and in order."

Article 31 contains two sentences:
1. on one's right to appeal.
2. on the binding force of decisions.

Re 1:

One of the fundamentals of church life is that the Lord Jesus governs His church by His Spirit and Word, i.e., by Holy Scripture.

The Scriptures are infallible.

Ecclesiastical assemblies, however, are not infallible.

Our churches do not use means of moral constraint in order to submit their members to their power and decisions.

Therefore there is a possibility of appealing against a decision taken by an ecclesiastical assembly, if it goes against the Scriptures.

Its introduction was really a matter of reformation. For the church of Rome states: In interpreting the Scriptures one may appeal against Scripture to the authority of the church.

An appeal may be made "if anyone complains that he has been wronged."

This sentence is carefully worded. It does not say: If anyone is wronged, but: If anyone is of the opinion that he is wronged. Here the freedom of the children of God is honoured.

By "anyone" we understand any individual church member. However, this does not exclude the minor assemblies from making an appeal.

It is a matter of course that prior to an appeal a request for revision may be made. This, then, is not expressed in Article 31, but one does have the freedom to act in this way first.

An appeal has to be made to the major assembly. For "the ecclesiastical way" has to be followed: from the consistory to the classis, from the classis to the regional synod, from the regional synod to the general synod.

It may be clear that such an appeal can no longer be made if the person or assembly concerned appeals years after the decision was taken by the minor assembly. The appeal must be made to the next major assembly.

The contents of a letter of appeal shall be:
1. the text of the decision against which the appeal is made.
2. the ground for the appeal.
3. the requested conclusion or decision of the major assembly.

Notice shall be given to the minor assembly concerning the appeal, preferably in the form of a copy of the letter of appeal.

While the case is *sub judice* — the appeal not having been settled by the major assembly — the execution of the decision has to be suspended. For if an appeal is made against a call extended to a minister, or against the appointment of an office-bearer, and the decision were to be executed, it would not make any sense to appeal: neither would it make any sense to include an article in our Church Order which would open the door to such an appeal.

Apart from this it may be clear from the second part of Article 31 that if anyone is of the opinion that the decision concerned was taken against the Word of God it cannot be binding to him.

Re 2:

The second part of the sentence of this article contains:
a. a rule.
b. an exception.

Ad a:

The rule is that a decision of a major assembly it to be accepted as settled and binding, even when it was made by a majority vote.

An unanimously taken decision is, of course, to be preferred, but this cannot always be reached.

Seeing the fact that there is an exception to this rule (on this exception itself see under Re b), everyone has the right to compare the decisions taken by a major assembly with the Word of God and with the Church Order.

For this activity the word "ratification" is sometimes used.

However, this may lead to misinterpretation and confusion.

The Dutch original of the Church Order's text as adopted by the National Synod Middelburg 1581 was accompanied by an official Latin translation. In Article 31 it has *ratum habebitur*, which literally means: shall be had as decided. The words "settled and binding" in the text of our current Church Order are a correct translation of this Latin phrase.

In other words, this article says that the churches have agreed to the acceptance as settled and binding of decisions taken by major assemblies. These decisions do not become binding as soon as a consistory or an individual church member would have formally "ratified" them. They are binding as soon as they have been taken (with the exception of "unless . . .," etc.).

It would be better to avoid the use of the term "ratification," which literally means: making something *ratum*, settled and binding. But that does not eliminate the right and the duty to examine the ecclesiastical decisions!

Ad b:

The exception can be a twofold one: a decision may be in conflict with the Word of God; it may also be contrary to the accepted Church Order.

Here again it becomes apparent: the Lord Jesus Christ governs His church by His Word.

The words "unless it is proved" do not mean: unless it is proved to the successor of the major assembly which took the decision — in the case of a request for revision — or to the regional synod and the general synod — when an appeal is made against a decision of a classis and regional synod, respectively — for inserting these lines in the Church Order would then have been as unnecessary as "forcing an open door"; the assembly concerned would immediately rectify the decision, so that a situation wherein a decision of a minor assembly would not be accepted as settled and binding would never occur.

The words "unless it is proved" have to be interpreted as meaning: proved to the interested person or minor assembly.

Here again our Church Order is of a confessional character, being in full harmony with Article 7 of the Belgic Confession of Faith, which says:

> We may not consider any writings of men, however holy these men may have been, of equal value with the divine Scriptures, nor ought we to consider custom, or the great multitude, or antiquity, or succession of times and persons, or councils, decrees or statutes, as of equal value with the truth of God, since the truth is above all.

It would appear that the contents of Article 31 can be summarized as follows: There is an opportunity of making an appeal when you feel wronged; but you have to accept the decision taken by the major assembly, unless. . . . The wording of this article might suggest that the whole matter is thereby finished.

This, however, would not serve peace and order. It would lead to independentism and even chaos.

In such a situation proof of a decision being in conflict with the Word of God or with the Church Order is to be given, either to a similar assembly — in case of a request for revision — or to a major assembly — in case of an appeal.

After one has gone the full "ecclesiastical way" — from the consistory to the classis, from the classis to the regional synod, and from the regional synod to the general synod — one has either to accept the latest decision as yet — which does not create any insurmountable difficulties whenever it is not a matter of conscience — or he has to "liberate" himself from the binding decision.

The latter way had to be followed when the general synod

of the forties in the Netherlands took decisions which were indeed in conflict with the Word of God and with the Church Order, and when they interpreted the word "unless" in Article 31 as "until" — which does not make any sense as we have shown in the above lines, and led to moral constraint.

ARTICLE 32. Credentials

Delegates to the major assemblies shall bring with them their credentials, signed by those sending them; they shall have a vote in all matters except those in which either they themselves or their Churches are particularly involved.

The latest revision of our Church Order no longer mentions "credentials and instructions." The word "instructions" and their tabling at a major assembly dates back to the days when there were no good mail connections, typewriters, and photocopiers. The agenda of the major assemblies were partly determined by these instructions, and often this prevented the delegates of the other churches from preparing themselves.

This deletion from the text of Article 32 does not make it impossible to a consistory to draw up instructions for its delegates to this classis. But this practice has to be limited to matters not requiring any preparation or study prior to the meeting — e.g. when the advice of the classis is required according to Article 68 of the Church Order, or when the classical churches are invited to send representatives to the ordination or farewell service of a minister.

A major assembly is a meeting of churches, not of individual persons.

The minor assemblies are present at them by means of their delegates.

These delegates do not attend the meeting as office-bearers, but as representatives of the assembly that sent them.

That they have been delegated must be proven by their credentials.

A letter of credence has therefore to be signed on behalf of the delegating consistory, classis, or regional synod.

It would be superfluous to refer therein to e.g. Article 31 of the Church Order, since these letters were signed by a Reformed consistory or a classis of Reformed churches!

A major assembly can only be declared constituted after the letters of credence have been investigated and it has become clear that all the churches, classes or regional synods are duly represented.

It is not desirable to mandate the delegates to vote in a certain way.

The discussion at the major assembly may bring some aspects of a matter to the fore that could not be considered by the minor assembly. The delegates must be left free to form their own opinion and vote accordingly.

Their letter of credence is the basis on which the delegates have the right to vote at a major assembly.

However, this right to vote is a limited one: They shall abstain from voting on matters which concern themselves or their own churches.

ARTICLE 33. Proposals

Matters once decided upon may not be proposed again unless they are substantiated by new grounds.

Time is "money" and even more than that, also in church life.

It would do harm to the Scripturally commanded "decency and order" if a matter would come up for discussion time and again. This can be done on new grounds only.

This new formulation, "unless they are substantiated by new grounds," made it unnecessary to maintain the old version, which said that instructions concerning matters to be considered in major assemblies shall not be written until the decisions of previous synods touching these matters had been read. (As for the word "instruction," we may refer to our comment on Article 32). For, in order to learn whether one has new grounds, the decisions of former major assemblies must be read.

This means also that the Acts concerned must be officially adopted by the assemblies themselves, and that they must be available to the churches.

By referring to "the assemblies themselves" we would like to emphasize that the Acts or minutes of a classis or regional synod should not be officially adopted by the next one, but by that meeting itself.

For first of all, the next meeting is often composed of different delegates. How would they be able to judge whether the Acts of the previous classis or regional synod are a true record of the proceedings? Furthermore, in such a case these documents would not be available in time for perusal by the local churches and their members. What is of greater significance is that the consistory is the only ecclesiastical assembly that has a permanent character. Every classis or synod, however, is a new one compared to the previous one. Therefore these assemblies should dispatch their business completely, which includes the adoption of their own Acts.

ARTICLE 34. Proceedings

The proceedings of all assemblies shall begin and end with calling upon the Name of the Lord.

A clause like this has had its place in the Reformed Church Orders since Emden 1571, on the ground of Acts 1:14 and 24.

There is no rule regarding the reading from Holy Scripture at the beginning of an ecclesiastical assembly. This is, however, a sound tradition.

ARTICLE 35. President

In all assemblies there shall be a president whose task it is:
a. To present and explain clearly all matters to be dealt with;
b. To ensure that every one observe due order in speaking;
c. To deny the floor to those who argue about minor things or who let themselves be carried away and cannot control their strong emotions;
d. To discipline those who refuse to listen.
In major assemblies the office of the president shall cease when the assembly has ended.

This article deals mainly with the task of the president or chairman.

First of all it sets out what this task includes:

a. He must clearly present those matters to be dealt with. To this end it is essential that he is informed in time, if possible, about incoming mail, and makes some study of difficult matters on the agenda.
b. He must see to it that the meeting is held in an orderly fashion. The discussions should not be disorderly. The best way is to hold discussions in one or two rounds, in which during the second round proposals may be expected from those who participate in the discussion.
c. He has to silence those who behave in a disorderly way.
d. If necessary, he must reprove them. Even at the ecclesiastical meetings all things should be done decently and in order.

In the second place this article deals with the duration of the position of the president.

It says that in major assemblies his office ceases when the assembly has ended.

Our churches do not have the position of a "moderator" or anything like that. They want to be on their guard against hierarchy.

As for the consistory's president, his position is regulated in Article 38.

ARTICLE 36. Clerk

Also a clerk be appointed whose task it shall be to keep an accurate record of all things worthy to be recorded.

We may repeat that the Acts of a major assembly must be adopted by the meeting itself, not by its successor.

As for the consistory, the next meeting can hear, discuss, and adopt the minutes of the previous meeting, in view of its permanent character.

"Press releases" should not necessarily include all sorts of particulars, as e.g. the opening and closing ceremonies, but inform its readers about the decisions taken and other essentials.

ARTICLE 37. Jurisdiction

> *The classis has the same jurisdiction over the consistory as the regional synod has over the classis, and the general synod over the regional synod.*

The major assemblies have been established also in order to act as arbiters, so that the peace of the churches may be preserved.

Article 37, then, is a sequel to Article 31. In matters of appeal and suchlike, the churches, by mutual agreement, have granted authority to the classis in respect of the consistory, to the regional synod in respect of the classis, and to the synod in respect of the regional synod.

This form of authority is fundamentally different from the authority the consistory has over the congregation — which is an "official" kind of authority, by virtue of the office of the office-bearers. That is why this article makes no mention of the authority of the elders over the congregation.

We repeat: The major assemblies are not "higher authorities." A major assembly is just an assembly of delegates from a larger number of churches. But this does not cause their authority to accumulate.

Meanwhile it may be clear that this article again is intended to prevent the churches from falling into the chaos and arbitrariness of Independentism.

ARTICLE 38. Consistory

> *In all the Churches there shall be a Consistory composed of the ministers of the Word and the elders who, as a rule, shall meet at least once a month. As a rule the ministers of the Word shall preside. If a Church is served by more than one minister, they shall preside in turn.*

After the "general" articles on the ecclesiastical assemblies the Church Order will now deal with them one after the other.

The first one concerning which a number of regulations have been made is the consistory.

Article 38 first of all says that in all churches there shall be a consistory, consisting of the minister(s) of the Word and the elders.

We have already learned from Scripture that the consistory is the only ecclesiastical assembly that was instituted by Christ's apostles (see Article 29). We referred to I Timothy 4:14, which speaks of "the council of elders" (*presbyterion*), suggesting that it is a body (see also Acts 20:17, 28; I Timothy 5:17; I Peter 5:1-3; cf. Matthew 16:19).

The consistory shall meet at regular intervals, at least once a month.

Furthermore, this article deals with the matter of who shall preside. The minister shall act as a chairman. "As a rule," for if there is no minister one of the elders has to act as president.

But in churches with more than one minister they shall preside in turn — e.g. each of them for a month.

ARTICLE 39. Consistory and the Deacons

Where the number of elders is small, the deacons may be added to the consistory by local arrangement; this shall invariably be done where the number of elders or the number of deacons is less than three.

Before briefly commenting on the contents of this article we would like to add something to what we read under Article 23.

There we touched slightly on the difference between Article 30 of the Belgic Confession of Faith and Article 36 of the Church Order in determining which office-bearers belong to the consistory.

The Confession speaks of

elders and deacons, who, together with the pastors, form the council of the Church.

The Church Order restricts the membership of the consistory to the ministers and the elders, and speaks in several articles of "the consistory and the deacons."

It is not our task to solve this "problem," but we would like to pass on a few lines from the report of the deputies for the revision of the Church Order, appointed by the General Synod Kampen 1975 of the Dutch sister churches. They wrote (our translation):

Art. 30 of the Belgic Confession of Faith clearly points *to the outside*, over against the hierarchical church government of the church of Rome and also over against the territorial idea of the government ruling the church. In order to preserve the true religion the Lord has ordained Ministers of the Word, elders, and deacons, and not popes, bishops, et al., as in the clerical hierarchy. This is the *spiritual* police, which has to be distinguished well from the *political* forms of government entrusted to the magistrates.

. . . From this emphasis on the *spiritual* police it is derived that the magistrates are told: the church has her own, spiritual form of government and therefore her own "senate" (council), different from your form of government and senate.

According to these deputies a development has taken place since the Belgic Confession was written, a development whereby the Church Order points *to the inside*, the internal life of the churches.

As for Article 39, we should realize that some congregations are only small; consequently the number of elders and deacons is also small.

The Church Order has made a provision in such a case: the deacons may be added to the consistory (it says: "may;" it is not compulsory). This can be arranged locally, but the churches have agreed upon it that this shall invariably be done where there are fewer than three elders or deacons.

The reason for including this article appears to be the danger that supervision and discipline — in the case of a small consistory — might be handled in a far too personal fashion, thus leading to partiality and arbitrariness.

It seems to us that the present rule in our Dutch and Australian sister churches must be preferred when it says (we quote Article 37 of the Church Order of the Free Reformed Churches of Australia):

> Where the number of elders and deacons is small the consistory can, on the basis of local rules, always meet together with the deacons.

> In that case, matters pertaining to supervision and discipline shall be handled with the advice of the deacons and matters pertaining to the office of deacons with the advice of the elders.

> This shall invariably be the rule if both the number of elders and the number of deacons is less than three.

For in that way, as the Form for the Ordination of Elders and/or Deacons (in the *Book of Praise* 1972, p. 533) states,

> the offices . . . remain distinct one from the other.

ARTICLE 40. Constitution of a Consistory

> *In places where the consistory is to be constituted for the first time or anew, this shall be done only with the advice of classis.*

The required advice of the classis does not mean that the initial or renewed institution is a classical affair. The desire to be instituted as a congregation has to live among the brothers and sisters concerned, and to be expressed at the correct place: to the consistory under the care of which they have been placed (Article 39). This assembly has to bring the matter to the classis.

The advice of the latter means that this body is of the same opinion, namely, that the time is ripe for instituting the offices.

It is a matter of course that the newly instituted church is immediately incorporated into the federation of churches.

As long as classis have been established, the synod will have to take the place of the classis.

ARTICLE 41. Places without a Consistory

> *Places where as yet no consistory can be constituted shall be assigned by classis to the care of a neighbouring consistory.*

At some places only a few brothers and sisters are living. Their number is too small for the constitution of a consistory. In such a case they shall be put under the care of a neighbouring consistory.

This makes them members in full rights of the congregation, the elders of which have supervision over them and must assist them.

The classis is mentioned because when this matter is dealt with in "the classical way" difficulties, such as e.g. boundary disputes, are avoided.

As a matter of course members-in-the-diaspora are expected to form a "house congregation" as soon as they can.

ARTICLE 42. Meetings of Deacons

> *When the deacons meet separately, as a rule once a month, to deal with the matters pertaining to their office, they shall do so with calling upon the Name of God. They shall give account of their labours to the consistory.*
>
> *The ministers shall acquaint themselves with the work of the ministry of mercy and, if need be, also may visit these meetings.*

The meetings of the deacons are not mentioned in the summing up of the "ecclesiastical assemblies" in Article 29, because they bear a distinct character.

That is why it is expressly mentioned that they, too, must be held "with calling upon the Name of God."

As for the execution of their office, the deacons are under the supervision of the consistory, just as each of the ministers and the elders are. Therefore they must give account to the consistory.

This does not mean that they have to inform the consistory about each separate case wherein they have supported one of the congregation's members or families.

"Labours" includes the handling of the funds they receive, the collections they need, and other affairs pertaining to their task, as it is described in Article 23.

The last sentence of this article aims at a close cooperation between the ministers and the deacons. Experience teaches that to the bearers of both offices it is very useful if the ministers from time to time visit the meetings of the deacons.

ARTICLE 43. Archives

> *The consistories and the major assemblies shall ensure that proper care is taken of the archives.*

It is often difficult to write the history of a local church or of the churches in general. And sometimes it is almost impossible to trace a certain document.

Therefore our churches, since the latest revision of the Church

Order, have inserted a special article on the archives.

It is to be hoped that in this respect both local churches and major assemblies will indeed observe the Church Order!

ARTICLE 44. Classical Meetings

> *The classical meetings shall consist of neighbouring Churches that respectively delegate, with proper credentials, a minister and an elder, or, if a Church has no minister, two elders, at such a time and place as were determined by the previous classis. Such meetings shall be held at least once in three months, unless the convening Church, in consultation with the neighbouring Church, concludes that no matters have been sent in by the Churches which would warrant the convening of a classis. Cancellation of a classis shall, however, not be permitted to occur twice in succession.*
>
> *In these meetings the ministers shall preside in rotation, or one shall be chosen to preside; however, the same minister shall not be chosen twice in succession.*
>
> *The president shall ask whether the ministry of the office-bearers is continued, decisions of the major assemblies are honoured, and whether there is any matter in which the consistories need the judgment and help of classis for the proper government of their Church.*
>
> *At the close of the classical and other major assemblies, censure shall be exercised over those who in the meeting have done something worthy of reproof, or who have scorned the admonition of the minor assemblies. At the last classis before regional synod delegates shall be chosen to that synod.*
>
> *If two or more ministers are serving a Church, those who have not been delegated shall have the right to attend the classical meetings in an advisory capacity.*

This article on the classis deals with the following subjects respectively:
1. what a classical meeting consists of.
2. the frequency of these meetings.
3. who will preside over them.
4. some permanent items on the agenda.
5. censure, if necessary.
6. the appointing of delegates to the regional synod.
7. advisors.

Re 1:

A "classical meeting" is not a meeting of "the classis," but of the churches of the classical region. "The classis" as a permanent body does not exist, the only permanent ecclesiastical body being the consistory.

This is why under Article 33 we saw that every classical

meeting must finalize its own agenda, including the adoption of its Acts or minutes.

These churches attend the classical meetings by means of their delegates: a minister and an elder, who are obliged to hand over their credentials (Article 32).

Vacant churches can delegate two elders. Small consistories can delegate a deacon if two elders are not available.

Re 2:

The meetings shall be held at least once every three months. However, there is an exception, made in view of the great distances between the churches, which would make the expenses too high if no matters of any importance are sent in by the churches. In such a case the convening church, after having consulted the neighbouring church, can refrain from convening the next classis at the appointed time. But this cannot be done twice in succession, for then no fewer than nine months would elapse before another classical meeting is convened.

At the end of every meeting the date and venue of the next classis shall be determined. However, it may happen that the appointed convening church is requested to call the churches together at an earlier time for the handling of an urgent matter. Most classes have a rule concerning such cases in their "Classical Regulations."

Re 3:

The ministers shall preside in rotation, but the meeting may also choose a president — which is done in exceptional cases only, e.g. when the minister to preside or his church is directly involved in a matter to be dealt with at that very meeting, e.g. an appeal or suchlike.

To prevent domination by one of the ministers it is a rule that the same minister shall not be chosen twice in succession.

The Church Order does not cover every possible case. Thus, if there is one minister only in a classical region, he must preside over all the classical meetings as long as the other churches remain vacant. And if all the classical churches are vacant, one of the elders-delegates shall have to preside.

Re 4:

Apart from other items on the agenda, which are determined by a number of articles in our Church Order — Articles 4, 5, 7, 8, 9, 11, 12, 13, 17, 21, 31, 32, 34, 46, 51, 68, and 71 — there are some matters that are permanent items on the agenda. These are usually summarized as "question time according to Article 44." However, these agenda-items are of the greatest significance. They clearly show that life within the federation of churches can be a great blessing, since the churches have supervision over each other and in that way are kept alive as faithful churches of the Lord Jesus Christ.

This "question time" has three elements:

a. first there is the question whether the ministry of the offices is proceeding (Articles 16, 22, 23).

b. then whether each of the churches honours the decisions taken by the major assemblies according to Articles 31 and 35 of the Church Order.

c. whether they need any help or the judgment of the classis in any matter — e.g. in cases of church discipline (Articles 68, 71).

Re 5:

During the meeting anyone who refuses to listen to the rulings of the president, in accordance with Article 35 c., must be disciplined, but it may also happen that at the end of the meeting Christian censure must be exercised over members, either because of their actions during the meeting itself or because they have scorned the admonition of the minor assemblies, classis having received a complaint about this.

"Censure" means here: admonition, reproof.

Re 6:

The appointing of delegates to the regional synod, at the last classis before this major assembly will be held, is usually done by ballot.

Re 7:

Ministers of churches with more than one minister have the right to serve the classical meetings as advisors even when they have not been delegated.

ARTICLE 45. Counsellors

> *Each vacant Church shall request to appoint as counsellor the minister it desires as such, to the end that he may assist the consistory in maintaining good order and especially may lend his aid in the matter of the calling of a minister; he shall also sign the letter of call.*

The churches live together in a federation of churches with the aim to assist each other whenever needed.

Normally there is a classical meeting every three months (Article 44). A vacant church, then, would have to wait for some time before she would be able to call a minister with the advice of the classis. In order to avoid such situations, the Church Order contains the provision of Article 43 concerning a counsellor.

The vacant church may make her own choice and request the classis to appoint him.

He will be able to serve the consistory with advice in all sorts of matters, but it is a rule that the calling of a minister will not take place without his advice, and that the letter of call must be signed by him.

This does not mean that it is compulsory for the consistory to ask for his opinion regarding the candidate or the minister to be called. His only duty is to see to it that the calling of a minister takes place "in good order" (see also Article 4).

ARTICLE 46. Church Visitors

> *Each year classis shall authorize at least two of the more experienced and able ministers to visit the Churches in that year.*
> *It shall be the task of these visitors to inquire whether all things are regulated and done in full harmony with the Word of God, whether the office-bearers fulfil the duties of their office faithfully as they have promised, and whether the adopted order is being observed and maintained in every respect; in order that they may in good time fraternally admonish those who are found negligent in any thing, and that by their good counsel and advice all things may be directed towards the edification and preservation of Christ's Church.*
> *They shall submit a written report of their visits to classis.*

This article on church visitation deals with the following points:
1. when, by whom, and where church visitation shall be carried out.
2. what it is all about.
3. its purpose.
4. report to the classis.

Re 1:
The visitation shall be carried out every year.

Visitors must be some of the more experienced and able ministers, appointed by the classis for this purpose.

All the churches of the classical region must be visited.

Prior to the visitation an announcement shall be made to the congregation, so that, if there are any difficulties not solved between congregational members and the consistory, these members may be given the opportunity to consult the visitors.

Re 2:
It is a custom that every classis adopts a number of guidelines for the church visitation.

These guidelines must include at least the following items:
a. the faithful execution of the offices, both individual and collective.
b. adherence to the sound doctrine.
c. the observance and maintaining of the adopted Church Order.
d. the promotion of the upbuilding of the congregation by word and deed.

Re 3:
The purpose of church visitation is:
a. in the negative: to admonish negligent office-bearers.

b. in the positive: to advise and assist the churches in promoting peace, edification, and well-being.

Church visitation can be based upon Holy Scriptures. Acts 11:22 tells us that the congregation at Jerusalem heard about the establishing of a church at Antioch, consisting of former gentiles. They delegated Barnabas, who — according to the original text — went by all the places where he could find Christians to speak with them, until he arrived at Antioch. Then is says:

> When he came and saw the grace of God, he was glad, and he exhorted them all to remain faithful to the Lord with steadfast purpose (verse 23).

So one congregation — that of Jerusalem — contacted the other — at Antioch — and the "church visitor" could be glad because he found a true Christian congregation and unity of faith between these two churches.

This, then, is the purpose of church visitation. The churches want to be assured that the sister churches are still showing the marks of the true church.

This is useful and even essential for life within a federation of churches, for then a consistory need not hesitate in a request for an attestation, because they know the church in question to be a faithful church. They also know that there is consensus in doctrine and church life between them and the other congregation. The same can be applied to invitations extended to a minister from another congregation; both the minister concerned and that congregation have the same basis of faith.

Church visitation, then, is of the greatest importance for the visited church, and consequently for all the churches.

Re 4:

It now stands to reason that the visitors are to report their findings to the next classis.

Acceptance of positive findings means the continued living together in the federation of churches, with mutual acknowledgment of one another as faithful churches of the Lord.

ARTICLE 47. Regional Synod

Each year some neighbouring classes shall send delegates to meet in a regional synod. To this regional synod each classis shall delegate four ministers and four elders. If there are three classes, the number shall be three ministers and three elders; if there are four or more classes, the number shall be two ministers and two elders.

At the close of the regional as well as of the general synod the time and place of the next synod shall be determined and the convening Church for that meeting appointed.

In case it appears necessary to convene a regional or general synod before the appointed time, the convening

Church shall determine the time and place with the advice of the classis or regional synod respectively.
At the last regional synod before the general synod delegates shall be chosen to that general synod.

At the moment there are two regional synods: Regional Synod East, to which the classes Ontario-North and Ontario-South send their delegates, and Regional Synod West, composed of delegates from the classes Alberta-Manitoba and Pacific.

As soon as another classis is established, the regional synod will no longer consist of eight ministers and eight elders but of nine each, every classis no longer sending four ministers and four elders but three ministers and three elders.

A regional synod composed from four classes shall have a membership of eight ministers and eight elders again.

Each regional synod shall determine the time and place of its successor and appoint a convening church.

This successor shall be held in a year's time, unless there are any circumstances which make an earlier convening necessary — in which case the convening church shall determine the time and place, with the advice of the classis to which she belongs.

The last regional synod before the general synod shall appoint delegates to this major assembly.

It is somewhat strange that this article on the regional synod already includes some regulations concerning the normal as well as early convening of the general synod — one of them even being repeated in Article 49.

ARTICLE 48. Deputies of Regional Synod

Each regional synod shall appoint deputies who are to assist the classes in all cases provided for in the Church Order, and — upon the request of the classes — in cases of special difficulties.
These deputies shall keep proper record of their actions and submit a written report on them to synod, and, if so required, they shall give account of their actions.
They shall not be discharged from their task before and until synod itself discharges them.

The major assemblies are held at regular intervals. Unlike the consistory, they are not of a permanent character, but between two classes, two regional synods, or two general synods certain matters must often be dealt with. For this reason these assemblies appoint a number of deputies, who are instructed to execute the matters assigned to them by these assemblies.

Article 48, however, deals with a special group of deputies, usually called "deputies ad Article 48" (or "ad Articles 48 and 71").

They are appointed to assist the classes in all cases provided for in the Church Order. These cases are mentioned in Article 5 (peremptory exams), Article 7 (examination of recent converts), Article 11 (dismissal of ministers), Article 12 (a minister entering upon another vocation), Article 13 (retirement of ministers), and Article 71 (deposition of ministers).

They are also appointed to help the classis, if invited, in other difficult cases.

These deputies have to record their actions and submit a written report to the next regional synod, and, if required, they can be called to attend synod to justify or further explain their actions.

This sentence shows us that these deputies are not rulers but the servants of the churches.

Only the regional synod can discharge them.

ARTICLE 49. General Synod

The general synod shall be held once every three years. Each regional synod shall delegate to this synod four ministers and four elders.

A general synod shall be convened before the appointed time if, according to the judgment of a regional synod, such appears necessary.

In the present situation a general synod consists of sixteen members, each of the two regional synods delegating four ministers and four elders.

Once every three years a general synod is held, unless, according to the judgment of one of the regional synods there are urgent reasons to have it convened at an earlier date, e.g. if another professor at the Theological College must be appointed. The "normal" time and place of the next general synod is, according to Article 48, determined at the close of a general synod, and its convening church appointed.

The draft agenda must be available to the churches at a predetermined date before the general synod commences, to allow various arrangements to be made. Deputies' reports must be forwarded to the churches, and the delegates must be given ample time to study them and the reactions from among the churches.

The way in which the agenda of the general synod is composed was discussed in connection with Articles 30 and 31; see also Article 50.

The binding character of its decisions was explained in Articles 31 and 37.

ARTICLE 50. Churches Abroad

The relation with Churches abroad shall be regulated by general synod. With foreign Churches of Reformed confession a sister-Church relationship shall be maintained as much as possible. On minor points of Church Order and ecclesiastical practice Churches abroad shall not be rejected.

The relations with foreign churches concern all our congregations, and must therefore be an item on the general synod's agenda.

Since our general synods appoint a "Committee on Relations with Churches Abroad," and these deputies have to report to the next general synod, this causes no problems.

The Canadian Reformed Churches are having Ecclesiastical Fellowship with The Free Reformed Churches of Australia, De Gereformeerde Kerken in Nederland and Die Vrye Gereformeerde Kerke in Suid-Afrika.

For this purpose they have adopted the following "Rules for Correspondence":

a. To take mutual heed that the corresponding Churches do not deviate from the Reformed Confession in doctrine, liturgy, Church government and discipline.

b. To forward to each other the agenda and decisions of the broader Assemblies and to admit each other's delegates to these Assemblies as advisors.

c. To inform each other concerning changes of, or additions to, the Confession, Church Order and Liturgical Forms, while the corresponding Churches pledge to express themselves on the question whether such changes or additions are considered acceptable. Regarding proposals for changes in the Three Forms of Unity, the sister churches abroad shall receive ample opportunity (at least three years) to forward their judgment before binding decisions will be made.

d. To accept each other's attestations and to permit each other's ministers to preach the Word and to administer the sacraments.

e. To give account to each other regarding correspondence with third parties (Acts 1962, Art. 139; Acts 1968, Art. 79, 6, b).

The Canadian Reformed Churches are a member of the International Conference of Reformed Churches (I.C.R.C.).

The last sentence of this article contains an old regulation. Every church has its own history of oppression and struggle against heresies and errors and of subsequent reformation. Every church also exists within its own cultural environment, and this has led to divergencies in church policy and liturgy.

Even the confessions and church orders may vary. However, in this respect there has to be a fundamental unity of faith.

The background of this article is what we confess in Article 27 of the Belgic Confession of Faith concerning the worldwide character of the church of our Lord Jesus Christ. (See also Heidelberg Catechism, Lord's Day 21 Q.&.A. 54.) Scripture teaches this in John 17:11, 17, 20, 21; Ephesians 3:14-4:6; I Timothy 3:15, 16 and other places.

We must also take to heart the apostle's admonition in II Corinthians 14:36:

> What! Did the Word of God originate with you, or are you the only ones it has reached?

ARTICLE 51. Mission

The Churches shall endeavour to fulfill their missionary task.

When Churches cooperate in this matter, they shall, as much as possible, observe the division into classes and regional synods.

The missionary task of the churches has already been explained in Article 18, where it said that the task of the ministers of the Word sent out as missionaries is:

in the specific region assigned to them or chosen by them in consultation with the Church that sent them, to proclaim the Word of God, to administer the sacraments to those who have come to the profession of their faith, teaching them to observe all that Christ has commanded His Church, and to ordain elders and deacons when this appears feasible, according to the rules given in the Word of God.

This makes it clear that the missionary task of the churches has been derived from the so-called "missionary command," issued by the Saviour (Matthew 28:18-20).

This is another article which — just like Article 18 — emphasizes that Mission work is not a task of individuals or of Mission Societies and suchlike; it is a calling of the churches.

The second sentence is intended to create order in the execution of this task: the churches shall cooperate along the lines of their division into regions.

This rule has been set, because today the ideal situation, in which each local congregation would fulfill its mandate by sending out a missionary, cannot be reached.

It is indeed observed in the work undertaken in Irian Jaya, Indonesia, by the church of Toronto in cooperation with other churches in Classis Ontario North; in Pernambuco, Brazil, by the church of Hamilton, in cooperation with other churches in Classis Ontario South; in Maragogi and São José, Brazil, by the church of Surrey, in cooperation with other churches in Western Canada; and among Canada's native Indians, home mission by the church of Smithers, in cooperation with other churches in Canada.

IV. Worship, Sacraments, and Ceremonies

ARTICLE 52. Worship Services

The consistory shall call the congregation together for worship twice on the Lord's Day.
The consistory shall ensure that, as a rule, once every Sunday the doctrine of God's Word as summarized in the Heidelberg Catechism is proclaimed.

Holy Scripture does not rule on the frequency of our Sunday church services. Our churches have, according to tradition, determined it at two, one in the morning, the other in the afternoon or evening.

The Bible does not contain a complete order of the service either. Many churches follow the order that was suggested by the General Synod Middelburg 1933 of the Dutch churches. Preference, however, should be given to the old liturgy — now also used again in the sister churches in the Netherlands and elsewhere — dating back to the days of the Reformation, in which the order of "the two great commandments" and that of "the Lord's Prayer" is obeyed: first the preaching of God's Word and the administration of the sacraments, only then the offerings and the intercessory prayers; that is, first the LORD our God and then things that are connected with "the neighbour." This order is reflected in the Heidelberg Catechism, Lord's Day 38. It is also apparent in the old prayer forms in the *Book of Praise*, 1984, pp. 641-647. (It would be wise to use these prayers more often in our church services!)

Catechism preaching has always had an important position in the Reformed churches.

The church of the Lord Jesus Christ is a confessing church. Her members have to know what she confesses and teaches. Teaching her members about her confession on a regular basis will be conducive to her spiritual well-being.

Catechism preaching is administration of God's Word in the full sense of the word. The many proof texts which a good edition of the Catechism contains show that the contents have been taken from the Bible. The Catechism summarizes the doctrine of Holy Scripture and obeys the Apostle Paul's command of II Timothy 2:2 that "the sacred deposit" shall be passed on to the coming generations.

The origin of Catechism preaching was a combination of what today is Catechism class and Catechism preaching. In the afternoon services first of all the young members of the congregation were given instruction. They had to recite part of the Catechism, from the youngest group to the oldest. The minister then explained to them a "Lord's Day." This explanation ended with a sermon in which the whole congregation was addressed.

Later on these two elements were separated, so that today

our youngsters normally have "Catechism class" on a weekday, while in one of the two church services Catechism preaching takes place.

The great significance of Catechism preaching becomes apparent when we compare the standard of preaching in those church groups that no longer have Catechism preaching or never did have it, with the preaching in our churches. The same could be done regarding the Scriptural knowledge of the average church member. We have every reason to be thankful to the Lord for this privilege.

Our churches would do wise to see to it that the regular Catechism preaching is not interrupted by all sorts of "specials."

For several reasons the old practice of Catechism preaching taking place in the afternoon service is no longer strictly followed.

ARTICLE 53. Days of Commemoration

Each year the Churches shall, in the manner decided upon by the consistory, commemorate the birth, death, resurrection, and ascension of the Lord Jesus Christ, as well as His outpouring of the Holy Spirit.

In the beginning of the Christian church there were no special public worship services besides the services on the Lord's Day. The congregation held her meetings, often early in the morning and in the evening. There was a festal celebration of the Lord's Supper as well. But there were no other festivals.

Later on the reformers of the 16th century, seeking to follow the example of the early Christian church, would have liked to abolish the many festivals other than the Lord's Day, as a reaction against the Roman Catholic practice which created all sorts of "sacred times." In 1520 Martin Luther sighed that the Lord's Day might be the only feastday. When John Calvin arrived in Geneva in the year 1536, he stressed from the very beginning the Lord's Day as the only feastday. Even the matter of the celebration of festivals was one of the reasons for Calvin's and William Farel's banishment. After their return the city council of Geneva instituted four feastdays: "Christmas," Circumcision Day, Annunciation (to Mary) Day, and Ascension Day. Work on these days was prohibited.

In Scotland John Knox abolished the special festivals.

As for the Reformation in the Netherlands, the Synod of Dordrecht 1574 decided that one had to be satisfied with only the Lord's Day. Synod approved of preaching on Christ's birth on the Lord's Day prior to "Christmas," of giving attention to Christ's resurrection in the sermon on Easter and to the outpouring of the Holy Spirit on Pentecost. However, these days must not be considered as being "higher" and more "sacred" than the Lord's Day.

The new version of the Church Order shows soberness in this respect. It does not speak of "festivals" but of "Days of Commemoration."

82

The inclusion of this article does not mean that our churches must strictly adhere to an "ecclesiastical year," with an "Advent" of four weeks and "Lent" with its seven "Passion Sundays," etc.

We do not "play" or repeat the great events in sacred history, but — just as this Article says — commemorate them!

ARTICLE 54. Days of Prayer

> *In time of war, general calamities, and other great afflictions the presence of which is felt throughout the Churches, a day of prayer may be proclaimed by the Churches appointed for that purpose by general synod.*

The contents of this article are a remnant of the ancient custom to appoint days of prayer and fasting, concerning which the magistrates had to be requested for permission because public life would come to a complete standstill on these days.

By having adopted this article the churches maintain order, so that in times of great difficulties a day of prayer is held in all the congregations at the same time.

Every synod shall appoint churches for the purpose of nominating such a day of prayer, if desirable.

Recent general synods have appointed the churches of Burlington-West and Edmonton-Providence.

It is remarkable that the Acts of General Synod Cloverdale 1983 (Article 175) speak of "Churches for Days of Fasting and Prayer." Fasting, however, is no longer mentioned in the Church Order!

ARTICLE 55. Psalms and Hymns

> *In the worship services the Psalms will be sung in the rhyming adopted by general synod and the Hymns approved by general synod.*

We may be thankful for the fact that since the days of the Great Reformation the churches are again "Psalm-singing churches." The Book of Psalms — the songs of the Covenant and of the Kingdom of God! — has been given back to the congregation.

The melodies of the Psalms have a long history as far as the "modes" are concerned. They have connections with the early church, the synagogue and even the temple!

Our churches do not take a negative stand regarding the singing of hymns — even the Bible contains a number of songs outside the Book of Psalms. In the meantime they acted wisely by adopting no more than sixty-five Hymns.

The publishing of the *Book of Praise, Anglo-Genevan Psalter*, Revised Edition, in the year 1984 was the crown upon the efforts to provide the churches with a really Reformed church service book. In several respects the heritage of the Great Reformation has been preserved by it.

ARTICLE 56. Administration of Sacraments

The sacraments shall be administered only under the authority of the consistory, in a public worship service, by a minister of the Word, with the use of the adopted Forms.

Now first of all an article follows that deals with the administration of the sacraments in general.

This administration must take place under the authority of the consistory — which means that no one can administer the sacraments on his own initiative, but that a minister must be authorized by the consistory that has the supervision over the congregation.

Our churches do not practice "private baptism," "emergency baptism," or the so-called "communion of the sick"; the sacraments have been given to the congregations.

Our churches have adopted a number of liturgical forms for this purpose, for doctrine and liturgy are closely related to one another. Our liturgical forms contain "the doctrine" of the various ceremonies. The congregation is always first of all reminded of what Holy Scripture teaches us concerning the ceremony that is to take place.

As a result supervision is to be executed not only over doctrine but also over worship.

In this article we have an example of that double supervision.

Our churches have deposited and expressed their belief concerning the sacraments in these forms in an even more extensive way than they have done in their confessional writings.

This was also a matter of reformation. According to the teaching of the church of Rome, baptism e.g. "automatically" washes away original sin, and faith has hardly anything to do with it.

This article is also aimed at the preservation of the Reformed character of our churches.

ARTICLE 57. Baptism

The consistory shall ensure that the covenant of God is sealed by baptism to the children of believers as soon as feasible.

We have now come to the articles on holy baptism.

The first one is on "infant baptism."

Its first part refers more or less back to what we confess in our Heidelberg Catechism, Lords Day 27, Q.&.A. 74, and in the Belgic Confession of Faith, Article 34.

No further comment is needed here.

We do not practice the administration of baptism in the family circle or in a special baptismal chapel, in the absence of the congregation. Holy baptism is the ceremony by means of which one is incorporated into the Christian church (Article 34, Belgic Confession of Faith).

The clause "as soon as feasible" excludes the introduction of special "baptismal Sundays." Historically it is meant to refer to the first church service after the birth of the children — which, in most cases, means: the first Sunday-morning service. During the first few centuries after the Reformation the administration of baptism to infants did indeed take place as soon as possible. This is proved by the baptismal questions, which were addressed to "the fathers and witnesses." Later on a different practice came into being, and the clause "as soon as feasible" caused some heated discussions between adherers of "early baptism" and of "late baptism." Wherever almost all the babies are born in a hospital and as a rule are released together with their mother within one week, there is no longer any cause for friction. It is clear that delay of baptism is wrong. We may not let the Lord wait, when He is ready to sign and seal His covenant to our children!

ARTICLE 58. Schools

> *The consistory shall ensure that the parents, to the best of their ability, have their children attend a school where the instruction given is in harmony with the Word of God as the Church has summarized it in her Confessions.*

One of the consequences of the promises given by the parents at the baptism of their children is that the ministers and elders have to see to it that the parents give their children an education that is in harmony with the doctrine of the church.

The accent lies here on the duties of the consistory in having supervision over the parents.

This includes school education.

We have to be very thankful to the Lord that He has enabled us to offer to the children of most congregations a truly Reformed education, at the primary and even at the secondary level, and that a Reformed Teachers College has been established at Hamilton.

ARTICLE 59. Baptism of Adults

> *Adults who have not been baptized shall be engrafted into the Christian Church by holy baptism upon their public profession of faith.*

When adults present themselves for baptism, its administration is preceded by their public profession of faith.

This does not mean that two Forms are to be read i.e. the Form for the Public Profession of Faith and the Form for the Baptism of Adults, for the answer to the questions of the Form for the Baptism of Adults is at the same time a public profession of faith.

The revised Church Order of the Dutch sister churches has here an additional sentence (in our translation):

> They are therefore called to celebrate the Lord's Supper and shall promise to do so when they are baptized.

Our churches have left such a sentence out of their Church Order, apparently because among them there are no difficulties in this respect.

ARTICLE 60. Lord's Supper

The Lord's Supper shall be celebrated at least once every three months.

The ancient Christian church used to have "the breaking of bread" at least every Sunday (Acts 2:42, 46; 20:7). At Jerusalem it even happened every day, until far into the second century, according to patristic sources.

Already in the early stages of church history the idea that the sacrament of the Lord's Supper was a sacrifice of man crept in. Soon afterwards it was accompanied by the theory of the transubstantiation of the elements of bread and wine, and their elevation. The celebration of this sacrament degenerated and became the Mass, with its character of a "show."

A consequence of the idea of a sacrifice was that the participation of the "lay people" was no longer an essential part of the Mass.

This led to the practice whereby the communion was reduced to a few celebrations per year. To many people "communion" at Christmas, Easter, and Pentecost was a maximum.

The Lateran Council, 1215, ruled that everyone had to partake in the communion at least once a year, at Easter.

This was also the result of another rule, dating back to the middle of the eleventh century, which said that at Christmas, Easter, and Pentecost the people had to offer a sacrifice for the financial support of the priests, but this prevented the poorer people from partaking in the communion except at Easter.

The above-mentioned dates were partly taken over by the churches of the Reformation.

We can furthermore say: They followed the frequency of the so-called *Gemeindekommunion*.

During the late Middle Ages there was some reaction against the character of the Mass as show. This led in places to the institution of separate communion services, namely in the South of Germany and in some regions of Switzerland. Consecration of the elements did not take place during them; the people made use of the elements that had been consecrated during the Mass, but full emphasis was put on the "communion."

This way a remnant of the Lord's Supper according to Holy Scripture was preserved: the participation of the congregation.

These *Gemeindekommunion* services were held at Easter, Pentecost, and Christmas.

The Reformers took over these dates of communion.

Although on more than one occasion John Calvin expressed his strong desire to return to the practice of the ancient Christian church, Reformed churches have never complied with his wishes. In his own city, Geneva, the civil magistrates strongly opposed his efforts, and in other important cities like Zürich and Bern, the usual practice was also maintained.

In the Southern Netherlands — today's Belgium — the churches agreed to a minimum of four times a year, in the Northern part of that country that minimum was set at six times. But later on four times was added as an alternative.

This, then, happened to be the rule of the old version of the Church Order: "The Lord's Supper shall be administered at least every two or three months."

The revised version of 1983 has reduced the minimum frequency to "at least once every three months."

Our churches have adopted an "Abbreviated Form for the celebration of the Lord's Supper," following the Dutch sister churches. But it is rather strange that the wish to have such a brief form came up in relation to the desire for a more frequent celebration of the Lord's Supper, while the "Abbreviated Form" is used "for the second service" wherein the celebration of the Lord's Supper is "continued!"

Its proper use would be promoted by the introduction of a monthly administration of the Lord's Supper — according to a compromise which William Farel and John Calvin proposed before they, in the year 1538, were exiled from Geneva. This celebration, then, could take place in only one of the church services, so that the "continuation" in the second service could be abolished.

The Church Order does not make mention of a "preparatory sermon," nor of a "thanksgiving service." Both preparation and thanksgiving are included in the form.

ARTICLE 61. Admission to the Lord's Supper

> *The consistory shall admit to the Lord's Supper only those who have made public profession of the Reformed faith and lead a godly life. Members of sister-Churches shall be admitted on the ground of a good attestation concerning their doctrine and conduct.*

Our churches do not know the practice of "the open table" at the Lord's Supper.

In some church groups every one is welcome who feels the desire to participate in the Lord's Supper. The responsibility rests fully on the individual.

According to what we confess, the responsibility also lies with the consistory, and indeed, with the whole congregation. This is why our Church Order contains an article on the admission to the Lord's Supper.

Admittance is granted to those who have learnt to "discern the body" of the Lord (I Corinthians 11:29), and therefore have made public profession of their faith.

For the same reason our churches do not practice "children's communion."

As for persons who want to join our churches and who made public profession of their faith in a church other than one of our sister churches, the consistory shall investigate whether they

confess that the doctrine of the Old and New Testament, summarized in the confessions and taught here in this Christian Church, is the true and complete doctrine of salvation (Form for the Baptism of Infants; cf. also the forms for the Baptism of Adults and for the Public Profession of Faith, *Book of Praise*, 1984, pp. 587, 591, 593).

The words in the first sentence "and lead a godly life" are added to keep the table of the Lord pure and holy by keeping away those who do not lead such a godly life even though they have made their public profession of faith.

The same necessary supervision has led to the introduction of the rule expressed in the last sentence of this article.

It may include those members of sister churches who move from these churches and join their "new" church. They are admitted to the Lord's Supper on the basis of the attestation issued to them by their former consistory.

It also includes members from sister churches who want to participate in the celebration of the Lord's Supper as guests. They are admitted when they can prove that they are "members in good standing" in their own congregation and that they have there been admitted to the Lord's Supper. This proof can be obtained by asking their consistory to issue to them a declaration concerning their doctrine and conduct.

Supervision regarding the admittance to the Lord's Supper belongs to what our confession (Article 29 of the Belgic Confession of Faith) calls the second and third marks of the true church:

It maintains the pure administration of the sacraments as Christ instituted them. It excercises church discipline for correcting and punishing sins.

ARTICLE 62. Attestations

Communicant members who move to a sister-Church shall be given an attestation regarding their doctrine and conduct, after previous announcements to the congregation, signed on behalf of the consistory by two of its members. In the case of non-communicant members such an attestation shall be sent directly to the consistory of the Church concerned.

There are two kinds of attestations:
a. concerning communicant members and their children.
b. concerning non-communicant members.

The former shall be handed over to the applicants, while in the meantime, it is proper that the consistory of the congregation concerned is informed.

The latter shall be sent to that consistory.

The difference between these two ways of issuing attestations lies in the fact that in the case of a non-communicant member the ''new'' consistory is requested to take this member under its supervision and discipline, while a communicant member makes this request himself by handing in his attestation to the consistory of the church in his ''new'' locale.

In actual fact, an attestation is nothing but a statement regarding the member's doctrine and conduct. It is not a permanent membership certificate.

This article clearly states that the request for an attestation must be presented for the congregation's approval, before it can be issued.

This means that an attestation has to be requested some time, say a couple of weeks, prior to one's departure.

The purpose of such an announcement is to give the other members of the congregation the opportunity to raise objections, if necessary.

ARTICLE 63. Marriage

The consistory shall ensure that the members of the congregation marry only in the Lord, and that the ministers — as authorized by the consistory — solemnize only such marriages as are in accordance with the Word of God. The solemnization of a marriage may take place either in a private ceremony or in a public worship service. The adopted Form for the Solemnization of Marriage shall be used.

Whereas the civil governments authorize ministers of religion to solemnize marriages on their behalf, and our ministers are under the supervision of the elders, the ministers are bound to the text of this article. Which means that they shall not solemnize marriages without the consent of the consistory.

The emphasis, however, is on the duty of the consistory. They shall see to it that the members of the congregation marry only in the Lord, and thus in accordance with the teachings of Holy Scripture.

This requires also the use of the adopted form, which — after having summarized the doctrine of Scripture on the married state — leads to the taking of the vows before the countenance of the LORD.

This article gives two options: marriage solemnization either in a private ceremony or in a public church service.

Even in the first mentioned case it would be wise to arrange the ceremony at such a time that the members of the congregation are able to attend.

The supervision of even the whole congregation over their

fellow-members also means that proper announcement are to be made in time.

During the early years following the institution of the Canadian Reformed Churches the "continental" practice of "Marriage Confirmation" was followed. This practice was introduced early in the nineteenth century by the "Code Napoleon" because of the separation of Church from State, whereby the church was no longer granted the right to solemnize marriages. This Code, however, was never adopted in the former British Empire. Since our ministers have been authorized as marriage celebrants, "Marriage Confirmation" is no longer practiced.

ARTICLE 64. Church Records

The consistory shall maintain Church records in which the names of the members, the dates of their birth, baptism, public profession of faith, marriage, and departure or death are properly recorded.

Although the contents of this article date back to the days when there were no registration offices for births, deaths, and marriages, our churches have maintained this article for their own purposes.

Registers concerning particulars of all members must be compiled and kept up to date.

ARTICLE 65. Funerals

Funerals are not ecclesiastical but family affairs, and should be conducted accordingly.

In the liturgy of the church of Rome there is an official funeral service complete with a special celebration of the Mass, a sort of a sermon and prayers for the rest of the soul of the deceased, while after having been sprinkled with "holy water" the deceased is buried in "consecrated earth." This is the historical background of this article.

John Calvin had some strong objections against "funeral services": in his opinion the deceased should not be brought to the church, but to the cemetery. He even objected against the saying of a prayer, because quite easily the deceased and his virtues could be put into the centre.

No objections can be raised against the local minister's conducting the funeral of members of his congregation. It belongs to his task to comfort according to everyone's needs (Form for the Ordination of Ministers of God's Word, in the *Book of Praise*, 1972, p. 527).

Burying the dead is a Biblical tradition. Cremation originates in heathendom, and is in contradiction with our belief that we "sow" our deceased until the day of resurrection (I Corinthians 15:42-44).

V. Christian Discipline

ARTICLE 66. Nature and purpose

> *Since Church discipline is of a spiritual nature and, as one of the keys of the kingdom of heaven, has been given to the Church to shut and to open that kingdom, the consistory shall ensure that it is used to punish sins against both the purity of doctrine and the piety of conduct, in order to reconcile the sinner with the Church and with his neighbour, and to remove all offence out of the Church of Christ — which can be done only when the rule given by our Lord in Matthew 18:15-17 is followed in obedience.*

Christian discipline is to be practiced:
1. by self-discipline: everyone has to examine himself;
2. by mutual discipline: the members of the church have to admonish each other;
3. by church discipline: admonition may lead to suspension from the Lord's Supper, and finally to excommunication.

As for church discipline, it is one of the marks of the true church that (Article 29 Belgic Confession of Faith)

> It exercises church discipline for correcting and punishing sins.

As Reformed churches

> We accept only what is proper to preserve and promote harmony and unity and to keep all in obedience to God. To that end, discipline and excommunication ought to be exercised in agreement with the Word of God (Article 32, Belgic Confession of Faith).

This is why our Church Order contains a special section on "Christian Discipline," wherein the various aspects and stages of church discipline are set out.

The first article informs us about the aim of discipline.

It begins by saying that church discipline must be exercised in accordance with the Word of God and to His honour.

In this matter the church must act in harmony with what the Scriptures in the Old and the New Testament teach us about the nature and purpose of discipline.

As for the Old Testament, we may refer to many places in the "books of the Covenant," Exodus 21-23 and Deuteronomy, and also in the book of Numbers (e.g. Exodus 22:18-20; Deuteronomy 13:6, 17:7, 19:19, 22:24, 24:7).

Regarding the New Testament we may mention the instructions the Lord Jesus gave to His apostles-to-be in Matthew, chapters 16 and 18 (verses 19 and 15-20 respectively), and to the writings of the apostles (e.g. I Corinthians 5:2); also to the gospel according to John (20:23).

Scripture as a whole teaches us the necessity of church discipline.

This may be clear to us when we read how the Lord Jesus in His "disciplinary sayings" referred to the Old Testament (compare Matthew 18:15 with Numbers 19:17; Matthew 18:16 with Deuteronomy 19:15), and how the Apostle Paul did the same (I Corinthians 5:2, 13 compared with Deuteronomy 17:7).

From the very beginning the LORD God wanted to preserve the purity and holiness of His covenant people. His honour is at stake when sin gets a foothold within His church.

A church without the administration of discipline, or a church that makes misuse of her authority to discipline (Article 29, Belgic Confession) must be an abomination in the eyes of God.

The purpose, then, of church discipline has been described above.

Our Church Order formulates it accordingly: the sinner, a person who lets his life be dominated by sin, has to be reconciled with God — sin disrupts the relation with Him — and with his neighbour — if he has sinned against one of the commandments of the "second table" of God's Law. And the offence must be removed from the church of Christ, either by the just-mentioned reconciliation, which is in the blood of Jesus Christ (I John 1:7), or by excommunication (Deuteronomy 17:7; 19:19). For the holiness of the church of Christ is God's own holiness (Isaiah 12:6; I Peter 1:16).

The last few words are further dealt with in our comment on Article 67.

ARTICLE 67. Consistory Involvement

> *The consistory shall not deal with any matter pertaining to purity of doctrine or piety of life that is reported to it unless it has first ascertained that both private admonitions and admonitions in the presence of one or two witnesses have remained fruitless, or that the sin committed is of a public character.*

Our Church Order is a Reformed church order. Over against the development that took place in the course of the centuries and which led to the "romanizing" of the churches whereby the power and authority was put into the hands of the "clergy," the churches of the Reformation returned to the Scriptures.

The Bible shows us how first of all every individual member of God's church is addressed in the Law of God when it says (Leviticus 19:18; Matthew 22:39):

> You shall love your neighbour as yourself.

and, in the negative (Leviticus 19:17):

> You shall not hate your brother in your heart, but you shall reason with your neighbour, lest you bear sin because of him.

This, then, is of the greatest importance for the life of the whole congregation. Its members bear mutual responsibility for each other (James 5:19,20):

> My brethren, if anyone among you wanders from the truth and someone brings him back, let him know that whoever brings back a sinner from the error of his way will save his soul from death and will cover a multitude of sins.

For this reason our Church Order first of all reminds us of the clear rule which Christ describes in Matthew 18, a rule which must be applied when someone has committed a sin not of a public nature.

The consistory shall see to it that this rule is obeyed. They are not entitled to deal with any matter that has not been dealt with by the members of the congregation in accordance with Christ's words. This implies also the duty of the consistory to teach, if necessary, the members of the congregation to honour this rule.

ARTICLE 68. Excommunication

> *Anyone who obstinately rejects the admonition by the consistory or who has committed a public sin shall be suspended from the Lord's Supper. If he continues to harden himself in sin, the consistory shall inform the congregation of this by means of public announcements, so that the congregation may be engaged in prayer and admonition, and the excommunication may not take place without its cooperation.*
>
> *In the first public announcement the name of the sinner shall not be mentioned.*
>
> *In the second public announcement — which shall be made only after the advice of classis has been obtained — the name and address of the sinner shall be mentioned.*
>
> *In the third public announcement a date shall be set at which the excommunication of the sinner shall take place.*
>
> *In case a non-communicant member hardens himself in sin, the consistory shall in the same manner inform the congregation by means of public announcements.*
>
> *In the first public announcement the name of the sinner shall not be mentioned.*
>
> *In the second public announcement — which shall be made only after the advice of classis has been obtained — the name and address of the sinner shall be mentioned and a date shall be set at which the excommunication of the sinner shall take place.*
>
> *The time between the various announcements shall be determined by the consistory.*

This article deals with the continuance of church discipline:
1. with the first disciplinary step: the denial of admission to the Lord's Supper.

2. with the last step of the procedure (or hopefully not the last one): excommunication.

Re 1:

There is a "non-disciplinary" denial of admission to the Lord's Supper, namely, when a certain case — e.g. a quarrel between two church members — was not solved in time.

However, this article deals with disciplinary denial only.

It is a matter of course that those who have been denied admission to the Lord's Supper are not entitled to answer the questions asked at the administration of the sacrament of holy baptism; neither are they allowed to participate in the election of office-bearers.

All this means that whereas one's rights within the covenant community has not yet been denied him by excommunication, their execution is suspended. Here there is a parallel with the suspension of an office-bearer, (who is still an office-bearer) but is not permitted to execute the duties of his office.

It is a matter of the consistory's being aware of its calling to keep the congregation of the Lord pure and holy and at the same time being long-suffering towards the sinner. There must be room for "numerous subsequent admonitions."

Re 2:

This first disciplinary action is an initial step indeed. For the consistory has to watch the sinner's reaction: Will he repent? Is it clear to him from this "provisional excommunication" — as the denial of admission to the Lord's Supper is also called — what will happen if he continues in his sin?

The accepted form extensively shows us the seriousness of the excommunication: The sinner is in the Name and authority of Jesus Christ our Lord declared to be

> excluded from the fellowship of Christ and from His Kingdom. He (she) may no longer use the sacraments. He (she) has no part any more in the spiritual blessings and benefits which Christ bestows upon His Church. As long as he (she) persists in sin, let him (her) be to you as a Gentile and an outcast. (*Book of Praise*, 1984, p. 612)

This shall happen only with the advice of classis.

This ecclesiastical assembly acts in a supervising capacity. Its judgment regarding the necessity to continue the procedure of church discipline has to be the same as that of the consistory.

To state that such advice of classis may be neglected if only it has been obtained, would be a perfect illustration of formalistic reasoning. By "advice" is meant: "the concurring advice," as in Article 71. Latin has: *ex classis iudicio*. An eventual revision of the Church Order could easily clarify the text at this point.

This supervision is voluntarily accepted by the consistory because of the serious character of church discipline: It is a matter of life or death! The consistory, entrusted with the authority by the King of the church, has to be absolutely sure that they are on the right track.

Excommunication is often called "an ultimate remedy" (see under Article 66). Surely, it is executed for the well-being of the congregation, but first of all for that of a sinner, who — because of it — may recognize that it is his own obstinacy which keeps him from partaking of Christ and all His benefits, and may — as yet — repent.

This article also deals with what must be done between the first and the "last" disciplinary action.

First of all it presupposes that the admonitions are continued, as may be apparent from the words, "If he continues to harden himself in sin."

Next, the three public announcements to the congregation are mentioned.

The form our churches have adopted for this purpose covers in its respective parts all the stipulations made here, whereby information is given about the above-mentioned attempts, the denial of admission to the Table of the Lord, and the many admonitions.

Three announcements are to be made:
1. the first one does not include the name of the sinner, in order to spare him.
   The element of patience and long-suffering and the desire that the sinner may repent as yet may be apparent.
2. the second announcement includes the name. But it shall be made after consent has been given by classis (see under Article 73).
3. the third announcement informs the congregation about the imminent excommunication.

From the first announcement on, the congregation is urged to pray for the sinner. From the second on, they are asked to admonish him.

And all this "if he does not repent!"

By making these announcements — the time lapses between them is determined by the consistory — the silent consent (= again: consensus) of the congregation is obtained: Excommunication is a matter of the whole congregation, for her own holiness is at stake!

The second part of this article is about the way church discipline regarding non-communicant members should proceed.

The sins of these members are not specified. They may consist of indifference and aversion to the covenant or even hostility to the service of the LORD.

The procedure is as follows:
The consistory has to admonish such persons. This is at the

background of the words "In case a non-communicant member hardens himself in sin." When these admonitions reach the point that the person concerned does indeed harden his heart, a public announcement is made in which the name of the sinner is not mentioned. This, too, is intended to have the congregation pray for him or her.

A second such an announcement is made after the advice of the classis has been obtained. It includes the name and the address of the person concerned, and the date at which the excommunication shall take place if there is no repentance.

The Church Order does not make any mention of a certain age. Not every youngster reaches the age of adulthood at a fixed time!

This means that the "good-Reformed" rule must be obeyed which says: Every case must be judged on its own merits. However, sometimes the sin of "scandalous godlessness" has led to excommunication at the age of 21, and indifference to the service of the LORD at the age of 30.

The terms "communicant" and "non-communicant members" on the one side and "excommunication" on the other, have only their sound in common. In order to prevent confusion it may be advisable to try to find other terms. "Baptized members" is not suitable either, because also the "confessing or communicant members" were once baptized!

The final sentence of the article regards the procedures concerning both communicant and non-communicant members.

The above-mentioned rule that every case shall be judged on its own merits means that no fixed time-limit between the various announcements can be set, and that this must be left to the discretion of the consistory.

Article 68 does not make mention of any forms for excommunication. However, they have been included in the *Book of Praise*, 1984, pp. 607-614).

ARTICLE 69. Repentance

> *When someone repents of a public sin or of a sin which had to be reported to the consistory, the latter shall not accept his confession of sin unless he has shown real amendment.*
> *The consistory shall determine whether the benefit of the congregation requires that this confession of sin shall be made publicly and — in case it is made before the consistory or before two or three office-bearers — whether the congregation shall be informed afterwards.*

Church discipline is aimed at the salvation of the sinner and the removal of the offence from the church of Christ.

In case of repentance after the consistory has started to add its admonitions, it shall accept the confession of sin if it is accompanied by sufficient signs of repentance.

It is the consistory's responsibility to determine whether the whole congregation will be informed about this confession.

This shall happen if the sin was of a public nature. If the offence was publicly committed, it must also be publicly removed from the church of God.

In civil courts a confession of guilt can be the ground for a conviction. Not so in the covenant life of the LORD with His people!

ARTICLE 70. Readmission

> *When someone has been excommunicated repents and desires to be again received into the communion of the Church, the congregation shall be informed of his desire in order to see whether there are any lawful objections.*
>
> *The time between the public announcement and the readmission of the sinner shall be not less than one month. If no lawful objection is raised, the readmission shall take place with the use of the Form for that purpose.*

Excommunication is the ''ultimate remedy.'' Although it does not happen very often, when a person in question does repent, and subsequently desires re-admittance to the community of the church, it may be seen as being a result of the ''ultimate remedy'' having been applied.

> He who conceals his transgression will not prosper, but he who confesses and forsakes them will obtain mercy (Proverbs 28:13).

This mercy includes the re-admission to the community of the body of Jesus Christ, together with all the benefits thereof, e.g. the joy of participating in the Table of the Lord.

The re-admittance procedure is a sequel to that of church discipline. The congregation is informed. Silent approval is obtained when no lawful objections have been brought forward. After a period of at least one month the person is re-admitted into the congregation by publicly confessing his sin, for the purpose of which the adopted form is used.

Undoubtedly this will create joy not only in heaven (Luke 15:7,10), but also within the congregation of the Lord Jesus Christ here on earth!

ARTICLE 71. Suspension and Deposition of Office-bearers

> *When ministers, elders, or deacons have committed a public or otherwise gross sin, or refuse to heed the admonitions by the consistory with the deacons, they shall be suspended from office by the judgment of their own consistory with the deacons and of the consistory with the deacons of the neighbouring Church. When they harden themselves in their sin or when the sin committed is of*

> *such a nature that they cannot continue in office, the elders and deacons shall be deposed by the judgment of the above-mentioned consistories with the deacons. Classis, with the concurring advice of the deputies of regional synod, shall judge whether the ministers are to be deposed.*

A special article has been included in the Church Order regarding discipline in relation to office-bearers:
1. in relation to ministers of the Word.
2. in relation to elders and deacons.

The difference in procedure is only the additional regulation regarding the ministers of whom the classis, with the advice of the deputies of the synod who were mentioned in Article 11, must judge whether they ought to be deposed.

The reason for this special regulation is that the ministers were also admitted to the ministry of the Word in the presence of deputies of the synod (Article 5; cf. Article 7). The federation of churches is involved in both cases.

However, in both cases — of ministers as well as of elders and deacons — the judgment of the consistory and that of a neighbouring congregation, appointed by the classis, is required. This, again, is a sort of ecclesiastical "safety valve," which is offered by the federation of churches because in serious cases like these no mistakes must be made, no injustice done.

The sins worthy of suspension or deposition are further defined in Article 72. Article 71 only refers to the rejection of the admonitions of the church and to being engaged in a serious sin.

The former means that the admonitions concerning secret sins (plural!) have reached a sort of rounding off. The latter are not necessarily public sins only — compare the illustration of the term "gross sin" in Article 72.

The church of the Lord Jesus Christ is to be kept holy!

ARTICLE 72. Serious and Gross Sins on the Part of Office-bearers

> *As serious and gross sins which are grounds for the suspension or deposition of office-bearers the following are to be mentioned particularly: false doctrine or heresy, public schisms, blasphemy, simony, faithless desertion of office or intrusion upon that of another, perjury, adultery, fornication, theft, acts of violence, drunkenness, brawling, unjustly enriching oneself; and further all such sins and serious misdemeanours that rate as ground for excommunication with respect to other members of the Church.*

Here a number of serious sins worthy of punishment by suspension or deposition of office-bearers are summed up.

False doctrine or heresy means: deviation from one of the teachings of the Word of God as confessed in the creeds and the Three Forms of Unity.

Public schisms: raising "discords, sects and mutiny in Churches," as the old Form for the Lord's Supper used to say (e.g. in the *Book of Praise*, 1972).

Blasphemy: mentioning God's name or speaking of Him in an irreverent way.

Simony: this term reminds of the story of Simon the Sorcerer in Acts 8:18-24. It indicates the sin of selling or purchasing a church office or another privileged position in church life.

Faithless desertion of office or intrusion upon that of another: the sin of forsaking one's office and entering upon another vocation without proper approval (Article 12, Church Order), and the sin of entering into another's office (Article 15, Church Order).

Perjury: transgressing the 9th commandment in its literal text, swearing a false oath.

Adultery: the sin of violating one's marriage vow, a transgression of the 7th commandment.

Fornication: illicit sexual relations.

Theft: the sin of stealing, as forbidding in the 8th commandment.

Acts of violence: the use of brute force.

Drunkenness: drinking alcoholic beverages in excess. General Synod Burlington-West 1986 deleted the word "habitual" in the text which was adopted at the General Synod Cloverdale 1983, because it considered "drunkeness" as such to be sufficient for suspension.

Brawling: disturbing church services, and other noisy quarrelling.

Unjustly enriching oneself: all dishonest gain.

All these sins cannot be tolerated in office-bearers, as may be clear from I Timothy 3:3, Titus 1:7 and other places in Scripture.

In addition of the last few lines means that not each or all of these sins would be grounds for excommunication with respect to other church members; however, others are. Consequently, church discipline must be administered in these cases after the office-bearer's suspension or deposition, in the way described in Article 68.

ARTICLE 73. Christian Censure

> *The ministers, elders, and deacons shall mutually exercise Christian censure and shall exhort and kindly admonish one another with regard to the execution of their office.*

To the "Supervision of Doctrine" belongs also the so-called *censura morum* or "fraternal censure."

This is exercised in particular in relation to the execution of the office of the ministers, elders, and deacons. They exhort and admonish each other in a brotherly manner.

Usually this "fraternal censure" is exercised prior to the administration of the Lord's Supper. This may be a good "timetable," but our Church Order does not mention any connection with the

Lord's Supper. The point, then, is not whether the office-bearers would be able to celebrate the Lord's Supper together, but whether they execute their office in a faithful way: they shall exhort and kindly admonish one another in this respect.

In order to prevent confusion it would be better to adopt a different "timetable."

ARTICLE 74. No Lording it Over Others

No Church shall in any way lord it over other Churches, no office-bearer over other office-bearers.

We may briefly repeat from the Introduction — under 6 — that in earlier days the present Article 74 used to be Article 1.

The Reformed character of our churches is expressed here: They live under the one and only universal Bishop and the only Head of the Church, Jesus Christ. Under Him no congregation is of greater importance than the other, no office-bearer is a higher authority than the other.

Even when the churches have agreed to do certain things in common or in the same way, and when they submit themselves to the supervision of the sister churches, and have created a certain form of jurisdiction in the federation of churches, this was a voluntary act of free churches in accordance with what Holy Scripture teaches us concerning the unity of the Spirit that must be maintained.

ARTICLE 75. Property of the Churches

All property, both real and personal, which belongs to the Churches comprised respectively in classes, regional synods, and general synods in common, shall be held in trust for such Churches in equal shares by deputies or trustees appointed for that purpose from time to time by the appropriate classis, regional synod, or general synod, and such deputies or trustees shall be bound by the terms of their appointment and instruction and are subject to being discharged by a subsequent classis, regional synod, or general synod.

This article has been included in the Church Order after the example set by the Dutch churches, which at their General Synod Middelburg 1933 adopted a similar text, in order to safeguard the common property of the churches.

It is no wonder, then, that it has been formulated in juridical terms.

General Synod Toronto 1974 adopted the present text on the following grounds (Acts Article 66):

"The old Article 84 Church Order does not legally safeguard the possessions of the Churches by proper general provisions."

ARTICLE 76. Observance and Revision of the Church Order

> *These articles, which regard the lawful order of the Church, have been adopted with common accord. If the interest of the Churches demand such, they may and ought to be changed, augmented, or diminished. However, no consistory, classis, or regional synod shall be permitted to do so, but they shall endeavour diligently to observe the articles of this Church Order as long as they have not been changed by a general synod.*

This final article deals with the Church Order itself.

It starts with a sort of solemn statement that "these articles, which regard the lawful order of the Church, have been adopted with common accord."

It is remarkable that this first sentence does not speak of "the Church Order" — as is done in the last line, — but of "these articles, which regard the lawful order of the Church." Here again we are reminded of the Scriptural foundation of our Church Order, I Corinthians 14:40: "All things should be done decently and in order."

Of course, any fruit of human activity is fallible, or inadequate in a certain situation. There is, therefore, room for amending, augmenting or diminishing all these articles, but this is a matter of the churches in general who have agreed to accept them.

This is why our Church Order also concludes with its last rule — adopted by all churches — that they shall diligently observe the provisions of this Church Order as long as they are not changed.

At the same time it may become clear why in Article 31 the possibility of a major assembly's decision being in conflict with the Church Order is mentioned as an exception to the rule: decisions of major assemblies are binding.

The statement made in the first lines of this article proves that it was an important moment in the history of the Reformed churches when at the well-known Synod of Dordrecht 1618/19 "The Church Order of Dordrecht" was adopted.

The same can be said about the day when the Canadian Reformed Churches decided to establish a federation of churches and to adopt "The Church Order of Dordrecht" (see the Introduction sub 9).

It can even be applied to the moment when on Wednesday, November 16, 1983, the General Synod of Cloverdale adopted the revised version of this Church Order (Acts, Article 91).

May the brief commentary, offered in this booklet assist the churches in the observance of this Church Order to the well-being of the congregations which have been bought by the blood of our beloved Saviour, the Lord Jesus Christ!